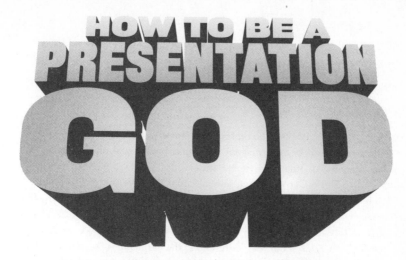

HOW TO BE A PRESENTATION GOD

Build, Design, and Deliver
Presentations that Dominate!

SCOTT SCHWERTLY

WILEY

John Wiley & Sons, Inc.

Published by John Wiley & Sons, Inc., Hoboken, New Jersey.

Published simultaneously in Canada.

For general information on our other products and services or for technical support, please contact our Customer Care Department within the United States at (800) 762-2974, outside the United States at (317) 572-3993 or fax (317) 572-4002.

Wiley also publishes its books in a variety of electronic formats. Some content that appears in print may not be available in electronic books. For more information about Wiley products, visit our web site at www.wiley.com.

ISBN 978-0-470-91584-4 (cloth); ISBN 978-1-118-01307-6 (ebk); ISBN 978-1-118-01308-3 (ebk); ISBN 978-1-118-01309-0 (ebk)

Printed in the United States of America

10 9 8 7 6 5 4 3 2 1

For Cara, you are my first fan and most important critic.

Contents

Foreword

Readers of my column and my blog know that the need to have regular human moments at work is similar to the need to stand up and stretch on an airplane: your well-being depends on it. On top of that, a workday with regular face-to-face contact is more energizing than a day full of contacts exclusively via computer and phone.

Working at the computer or talking on the phone for a long time is as exhausting as staring at the TV. The brain starts to crave rest from input overload and fuel from human contact.

So when you're feeling tired at work, try creating a human moment for an energy boost. It doesn't have to be earth-shattering and intimate. It can be short and professional. You just need to be paying attention.

Even better: use all those meetings you have every day to create your own opportunities for such human moments. Scott's giving you the driver's license crash course right here—he'll show you how to speak like you want to change the world. He's got monsters to fight, and you get to be the hero. Use what Scott explains so well to connect with just one person in the audience (maybe that attractive one from Accounting). Just look him or her in the eye, right? That's the usual advice.

But it's so hard to look someone in the eye. Especially if you don't have confidence from knowing what you're doing up there. And most public speakers are not particularly naturally engaging. That's why going after just one person is a great way to test yourself—to see if you're really connected—by forcing yourself to look at one single person while you make a point.

This is a way to know for sure if you are connecting with your audience when you talk. Sticking with one person for each point is painful and nearly impossible if you are not truly connecting your material to that person.

But what do you do when you see you aren't connecting? Some people ignore it or trick themselves into thinking there is a connection: Think about all the deadly PowerPoint presentations you've sat through where the speaker was oblivious to boredom. Or just read on—Scott makes a great read out of all the time you've wasted on the bad presentations you've suffered through.

Comedian Esther Ku says the best thing to do when you can tell you're not connected is to acknowledge it. "If a joke fails, I poke fun at myself so I show the audience that I'm aware of what's going on." The audience doesn't need constant genius; the audience needs to know you are clued into how they are reacting.

After you've absorbed what Scott's offering here, you'll seem like a constant genius, a presentation god, ready to connect, because you'll have stopped wasting the audience's time.

You'll be focused on just one person and thereby connect with everyone. And most important, you'll have learned to respect yourself and your audience. What more can you ask from such a human moment?

—Penelope Trunk
www.penelopetrunk.com
Founder of Brazen Careerist

Acknowledgments

A BIG THANK YOU!

I want to thank my family, my clients, Kristina Holmes (my agent), the great folks at Wiley (Lauren, thanks for the opportunity!), and everyone at Ethos3. I also want to give a special shout-out to Brandy Nicks, who designed all of the illustrations in this book. Brandy has been with Ethos3 almost since the beginning. Without her presentation design skills, Ethos3 wouldn't be the great company it is today. Also, a big thanks to Josh Roberts, who helped me fine-tune my content. His contributions have been priceless. And most importantly, I want to thank you for taking the time to read this book. I hope it has empowered you to change the world with your next presentation!

Here's a list of some of the people (dead and alive) who have inspired me along the way:

Steve Jobs

Guy Kawasaki

Garr Reynolds

Budd Hebert

Nancy Duarte

Dutch Hoggatt

Michael Hyatt

Steve Yzerman

Bert Decker

Austin Smith

Ms. Housley

Seth Godin

Harry Beckwith

Abraham Lincoln

Bruce Lee

Marcus Buckingham

Tony Robbins

Tony Horton

Cliff Atkinson

Hal Higdon

Harry Truman

Patrick Henry

Larry Lessig

Daniel Pink

Scott Bedbury

Emil Zatopek

Matt Bellamy

Dale Carnegie

Jerry Weissman

Napoleon Hill

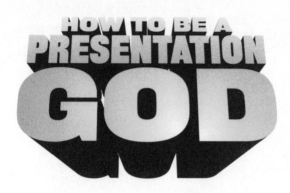

Chapter 1

A Killer in Our Midst

French writer and Nobel Prize winner André Gide once said, "Society knows perfectly well how to kill a man and has methods more subtle than death." Subtlety, thy name is PowerPoint.

What is it about bullet points that makes the human soul curl up into a ball of fetal terror? Why do fonts like Comic Sans and Papyrus sear the retinas so badly? How can so-called "experts" speak at length about the logistical applications of advanced financial modeling yet fail to zip up their pants?

Most importantly, when are we, the victims, going to work up the courage to stand up and walk out, taking as many reeling audience members with us as we can? We should be disturbed. No—we should be *outraged*. Time—both yours and mine—is being wasted.

As the CEO and founder of the presentation design and training firm Ethos3 Communications, I set out to answer questions like these some years ago. I want to make the unjust world of presentations just again. Here's a staggering statistic: 30 million presentations are given daily in human society. *Daily*. With that much hot air entering the atmosphere every day, we must either cap and trade public speakers or revolutionize the way presentations are given. Since we don't have a way to safely store public speaker emissions yet, I vote for the revolution.

On one hand, our society has embraced the presentation as a necessary element of doing almost any kind of business—selling, producing, distributing, organizing . . . you name it. On the other hand, presentations are universally mocked as one of the least productive elements of business life—more so, even, than smoke breaks. Would-be audience members rifle through medical texts as they search for a way out. Unlucky attendees pore through religious tomes in a hunt for salvation. Despite the fact that we have mastered the art of entertainment—DVR, the iPad, and the ever-expanding capabilities of the Internet that have put happy diversions at our fingertips—we somehow can't quite seem to put together 17 minutes of meaningful information in an entertaining, influential format. PowerPoint has degraded, rather than elevated, the art of the presentation. We are all fleeing in the wake of this disaster.

As a result, the art of concealed distraction has advanced beyond the wildest dreams of a high school class clown. I've seen how adept many of you are with your smart phones. Once, in a close-quartered presentation, I witnessed an audience member tapping out an e-mail on a BlackBerry with his big toe. I couldn't blame the guy: we were confronting our very mortality as we gazed upon a mind-numbing chart designed in Excel. I, too, felt the need to reach out to loved ones in that moment of crisis. I know in my heart that there was a purpose for that presentation, just as I believe that all presentations have a purpose. But as it

THE
SMOKE
MONSTER

If you're not careful, **Ms. Smoke Monster** will ensnare you in dangerous cloud of smoke breaks and other antics. Her goals is to get you off task and off schedule. BEWARE!

came to a close, I, along with every other attendee, walked away in bewilderment. Despite rapid advances in technology and psychology, few presenters are capitalizing on their presentation opportunities.

John F. Kennedy—a powerful presenter in his own right—once remarked, "The only reason to give a speech is to change the world." Of the 30 million presentations being given each day, how many do you think *actually* change the world? Better yet, how many presenters even set out to try? I understand that the third quarter budget approval meeting may not lend itself to epic prose and lectern-pounding passion; however, that doesn't mean that we have to read off a lifeless litany of figures in monotone without ever looking at the audience, as if to say, "I quite literally hate my life right now and resent the audience for being in any way associated with it." These are real human lives we're talking about. I firmly believe that a poorly planned, poorly delivered presentation represents a serious and threatening disregard for human life. We ought to present as though our audience only has two hours to live—one of which will be taken up by our presentation. How can we quickly and powerfully distill exactly what must be communicated so that they can get on with their goodbyes?

The reality for both audiences and speakers is that a presentation that does not move *something*—be it people, products, ideas, or values—is merely wasted time.

It is 20, 40, 60, even 90 minutes of real, living hours that are just thrown away. That's time that could be spent calling mothers,

A PRESENTATION THAT DOES NOT

MOVE

SOMETHING—

BE IT

people, products, ideas, or values—

IS MERELY

WASTED TIME.

brushing teeth the right way, or just staring blankly at walls or clouds rolling by. It would be far nobler to set the bored masses free than to burden them with yet another presentation filled with information they already know and that is being presented with a level of energy reminiscent of an old, lazy, spineless Raggedy Ann doll and not the cartoon version that moved.

The opportunity to speak before an audience always represents a significant opportunity, notwithstanding the dismal state of most presentations and the time they waste. Each time a group of individuals gathers to listen, they set aside self-absorbing thoughts and, for a brief moment, are forced to think collectively. Just being part of an audience has this effect on the human mind. Presentations by nature call us to think on a bigger scale— one beyond personal limitations. They compel us to become greater than the sum of our parts. Most presenters defuse this power almost immediately by choking on a sip of water, telling a horrifically cliché joke, or opening the presentation with, "If you'll look at the pie chart on page 2. . . ." Everyone—and I mean *everyone*—is capable of doing better.

Think of FDR's fireside chats and of speeches such as Winston Churchill's *Fight Them on the Beaches* and Dr. Martin Luther King, Jr.'s *I Have a Dream*. Throughout history, presentations have moved large groups of frightened, embattled, and disenfranchised people to decisive action. These speeches did, indeed, change the world, but the scale of those opportunities is not our focus. Intention—the effort and preparation we bring to the moment—is paramount. For too long, I've watched presenters sell themselves, their messages, and their audiences short because the stakes were not high, or not high enough. If we are going to leave our mark on the world, we must begin where we are.

I'm not asking you to sell all of your belongings, grow a ZZ Top beard, and hit the New Age circuit, exhorting all who will listen to begin sharing each meal with abandoned kittens. If you're willing, that would be a truly nice thing to do for society and could seriously curb obesity trends while addressing our nation's feral kitty problem. However, feline-related karma reserves are not the scope of this book. This book is written to help you utilize presentation opportunities more effectively—plain and simple. Despite the fact that technology, psychology, and the business environment have changed drastically since the introduction of PowerPoint, few presenters have adapted their craft to this altered environment.

Ironically, great men and women have been changing history and the world for thousands of years without the aid of a Microsoft or Apple software suite. Technological tools should augment—not detract from—our presentations. Remarkable presenters build trust, win people, and deliver results; these are the speaker's mandates. People follow people worth following, and people become worth following when they exhibit qualities that every human being is inclined to admire and covet—passion, energy, and direction.

The concepts in this book will help you design, build, and deliver seriously effective presentations. But there is one thing the concepts in this book cannot do: make you extraordinary.

Every presentation serves its master. The limitations of your personal hopes, dreams, and aspirations are the biggest inhibitor—or facilitator—of the presentation success you will encounter. Therefore, before we delve into content, design, or delivery, let's take time for introspection and ask ourselves: Are we worth following?

Do we possess the attractive qualities of passion, energy, and direction or are we waiting for some opportunity to come along that justifies the effort to be great? Today's speech may be routine information on home warranties at the local Rotary club, but who knows where that could lead? The only way *not* to find out is to give a lackluster presentation.

Be extraordinary. It's a tall order—one that I often forget to strive for myself. Not too long ago, I learned a trick that helps me focus: at the beginning of each day, I put five pennies in my right pocket. Since there's nothing a penny can buy anymore, I don't have to worry about accidentally spending them or being mugged. Each time I do something extraordinary, or just a little beyond my routine, capacity, or comfort zone—calling an old friend, helping a stranger, getting flowers for my wife for no reason—I move a penny to the left pocket. A complete migration of pennies from right to left reflects a truly meaningful day, one worth emulating tomorrow. Do this daily and watch the fruits of your life compound. Make it a lifestyle and you can comfortably lead people wherever you are going.

The extraordinary life may seem tangential to the requirements of the average presentation, but nothing gives information a

LIFE rewards COMMITMENT:

COMMIT TO BEING

great

AND

YOU WILL BE.

sharp edge like a driven human being. The sole objective of *any* presentation is to initiate change in a certain direction chosen by the speaker. Moving people is easy: Show them Pauly Shore movies and you'll move them quickly to the doors. Moving people to work harder, think broader, or invest their resources in you are more difficult tasks that require planning, creativity, and execution for their achievement.

Life rewards commitment: Commit to being great, and you will be. If you commit to change the world, you will. In the following chapters, I'll go over my own methods for creating presentations that dominate. These methods will allow you to put a powerful edge on your message. I've helped hundreds of presentations go from disturbing to earth shaking over the years; I want to see more earth shaking. But *you* have to bring the passion and the vision. How big is your dream? Where are you going?

Powerful presentations have a way of putting life into hyperdrive. Can you handle that? Are you ready to put a little more in to get a lot more out? If so, it's time to join the Presentation Revolution.

Chapter 2

Won't "Good Enough" Do?

The digital age has made countless artifacts from the twentieth century obsolete: typewriters, steam engines, home cooking, and personal relationships, for example. Perhaps the first individual to live a complete life without interacting with another human being has already been born. That individual will bank online, tickle a kid sister through the "poke" feature on Facebook, and telecommute exclusively. Oh, the wonders of the modern age!

The average presenter seems to be banking on such a future, hoping and praying that the day will come when he or she won't have to depend on social interaction and can instead rely on the cold, hard data they keep plastering all over the projection screen. Though empirical evidence is valuable, it is also uninspired; we don't buy our food based on algorithms that measure the caloric and nutritional content of a food against price per pound. We buy what we like, or what we are convinced will make Brazilian-cut Speedos and bikinis look good on us.

Audiences are composed of human beings who think on these terms. Our highly evolved brains have an enormous capacity for learning, interpreting, and incorporating data into our lives.

Instead of doing so ourselves, we generally let our hearts or appetites guide the bulk of our decision-making. Thus, when we ascend the stage to address an audience, variables that are obviously unrelated to the matter at hand—whether the shoes are shined or not, whether a slide has a funny picture or not, whether the speaker is kind, or smart, or inspiring—begin to have a direct impact on whether or not we will be successful in our presentation, regardless of the truth.

It takes a whopping *seven seconds* for the human brain to rifle through hundreds of relevant and irrelevant variables to form impressions about the people we meet every day. Since the average person reads about four words per second, by the time you finish reading this sentence, you could have reached an unshakable conclusion about another person—just like that. In less than seven seconds, I have decided that you are reading this book on your iPad in a coffee shop, so I want to give you an assignment: look around. See that girl? Hippie, right? See that guy? He looks rich. That little girl? Seems like a fussy toddler, probably. I may be wrong in my assumptions—after all, you may be reading this in paperback form in bed—but I proceed as if they are. The truth matters less than what I think.

It's completely unfair, but your audience is doing the same thing to you. They give you seven seconds to create your first impression, a reality that is shaped not by facts and figures but by emotions and abstract motivations. Empirical evidence is valuable; it is important for many of us to *feel* as if we've made up our minds based on data. However, we have formed our solid opinions in roughly seven seconds, so we know this cannot be true.

Can you build a case empirically in seven seconds or less? Chances are that you cannot.

The human mind is designed to function in this way. It's adaptive. It helps us take in and manage the incredible volume of information that is swirling about at any given moment, even when we're just blankly staring at walls. We have to take into account that our employees, customers, shareholders, and fellow citizens are taking an equal amount of time to form impressions about our companies, products, strength, or vision. What have you been doing with the first seven seconds of your presentations? If the words, "warm up," "open up PowerPoint," or, "tell my mom I have to go because I'm presenting, *now*," come to mind, then I am so glad you have decided to read my book.

Perception is everything. Facts shape realities, but oftentimes what people think about something colors the way it actually is. The conclusions being jumped to in the first seven seconds of 30 million presentations every day are like concrete: Though they are not necessarily permanent yet, they will be—very, very soon. My personal vision for the Presentation Revolution is not thousands of speakers rifling off their most explosive material in a seven-second period of time, spewing humor, sadness, enthusiasm, and joy like a five-course meal pureed into an unbearable eight-ounce beverage to be chugged. Rather, my vision involves an army of skilled professionals thinking critically about how best to utilize their time on stage. Presentations matter because you get to shape and mold perception before the concrete sets.

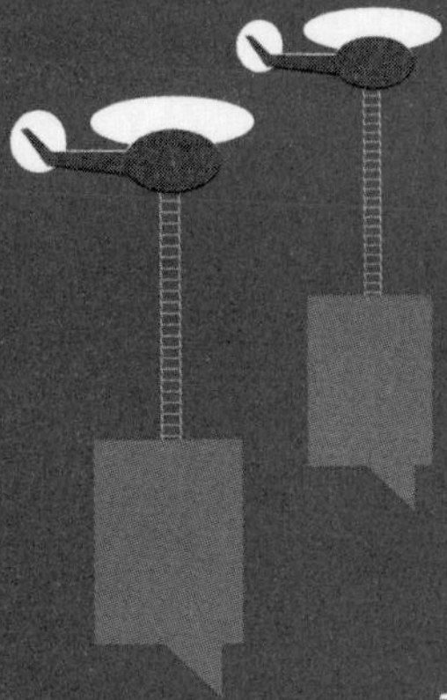

Presentations

MATTER

BECAUSE YOU GET TO

shape & mold perception

BEFORE THE

CONCRETE

SETS.

But far more important than your presentation is an expensive product, such as an MBA from Harvard and Ph.D. from MIT or a spotless record when it comes to supporting house resolutions supporting baseball and apple pie, right? Unfortunately, while innovative, smart, and spotless individuals are obsessing over their products, brains, and records, the pantheon of presentation gods—individuals who have made managing perception a sainted virtue—are eating their lunches. Let's look at some examples:

- At Apple's 2010 Worldwide Developers Conference, CEO Steve Jobs presented the iPhone 4 to the public. AT&T had to stop taking orders almost immediately thereafter. Is the iPhone 4 so fundamentally valuable that broke college kids should forego textbooks and pizza for weeks on end to have one? Probably not. But do they? Yes.
- Dick Hardt gave an impressive presentation at the O'Reilly Open Source Convention in 2005 that propelled his company, Sxip Inc., Identity 2.0 theory, as well as his personal brand into near-global recognition within the tech industry. A star was born in the course of a keynote address. Did other brilliant people have other visions for the future of identity in the digital age? Of course. In the wake of Hardt's presentation, did these visions have a chance? Probably not.
- Randy Pausch, whose *Really Achieving Your Childhood Dreams* presentation became the *New York Times* bestselling book *The Last Lecture*, witnessed first-hand the rocket-like trajectory that a good presentation can put you on. Was it a brand new idea, never before heard in human history? We know that there are no new ideas. Did he become the face of the philosophy and personally embody the message for the rest of his life? He did, indeed.

Sure, Apple makes a great product, Dick Hardt is a widely recognized genius, and Randy Pausch delivered content that changed people's lives. But let's be serious: There are always competing products, smart people, and great ideas. Talk to technology experts and they'll tell you there are computers, even phones, that can beat Apple products. Apple's products are fantastic; I am a zealous Mac addict myself. However, I'm well aware that while its technology is innovative, Apple is far more innovative in controlling the *perception* of the Apple brand. Jobs, Hardt, and Pausch recognize the effect perception has on their work. Their presentations matched the opportunities.

Presentations matter. The average human lives to be 78 years old. We spend the first part of our lives in school, the middle part working, and the end doing anything *but* attending presentations. We have approximately 40 to 45 working years to use our educations to determine what we think about everything. None of us has the time for such a monumental task—especially not by conducting a thorough review of the facts and figures associated with any one given topic. Presentations tell us what to think, and we are happy to rely on this service.

Controlling your presentation, then, is a vital aspect of controlling your message and, more importantly, what people think about it. Everything comes down to the presentation: Newer, better, cheaper products are always just a moment away. There is always someone smarter; there is always someone better. Superiority in the digital age is fleeting, if achievable at all. Developments and improvements leapfrog over each other daily, even hourly.

THE
best thing
ABOUT **PRESENTATIONS**

is that there is a

DEFINITIVE
STANDARD

FOR EACH ONE,

an action point
THAT LETS YOU KNOW IN

REAL-TIME

whether or not it
WORKED.

If you want success that lasts longer than a Facebook status, you absolutely must master perception.

The best thing about presentations—unlike products, brains, and records—is that there is a definitive standard for each one, an action point that lets you know in real time whether or not it worked.

Capital may be raised, products sold, representatives elected; in short, something occurs after the presentation that is directly attributable to the performance. A great presentation tells audience members a simple message: "I understand you. I understand myself. I know exactly where to go. You should follow me." If that sounds powerful, imagine what a bad presentation can do.

The fact is that most presentations—commercials, speeches, one-on-one interviews, and so on—are almost always lackluster. The percentage of people "on top" correlates with the percentage of people giving good presentations. You might be smarter than your boss, but does your boss present better than you do to his bosses, clients, and employees? Maybe you can sell a chocolate bar better than Willy Wonka, but how would Hershey's know? At some point, we have to face a simple, frightening fact: We control perception, or others control us. Leave it to others, and they'll spend seven seconds deciding the outcome of your life.

A poor presentation demonstrates an occupational death wish in a way that punching your boss in the face cannot even match; while punching your boss in the face controls perception (albeit it the perception that you cannot be trusted because you randomly hit people), a poor presentation does nothing at all.

Start thinking critically about what others are presenting to you: the commercials you watch on TV, the ads in the newspaper, your kids when they ask for the car keys. Is the message prepared, strategic, and informed? Does it make you believe something, do something, *feel* something? Effective presentations are conversations, even if it is one person on stage, holding a microphone and talking the entire time. Resonance—that singular feeling where individuals suddenly begin traveling in the same direction—is born out of empathy and preparation. It is not fate; it something that's achieved through hard work.

Our presentations, in other words, serve as a replacement for one, much bigger thing: our entire lives. I cannot drag an audience through a comprehensive personal history when I'm presenting. I have as little as 10 minutes to create an impression in their minds that fills in the gaps and conveys details about years of personal and professional qualifications that I simply cannot list.

Perception is the great equalizer in business and in life. On the perception playground, dumber, less experienced, or less responsible people all of a sudden have a very real opportunity to compete with the smartest, most experienced, most responsible members of their field. This is why we hear stories of brilliant innovators with hearts of gold wallowing in poverty while veritable idiots walk away with prize business. I'm not saying it's great; I'm just saying it's so.

The sooner you accept the fact that success depends on the perception of qualifications more than any qualifications themselves, the sooner you can begin to protect and advance yourself.

THE
FAKE
QUEEN

Externally, **the Queen** appears to have it all — good looks, a fancy dress, and fresh breath. However, if you look under her dress you will quickly realize that perception is everything.

Certainly, having qualifications in a given field makes it easier to give the impression that you have them. At the end of the day, we all want to work with experts and the best in the industry. But there's just not enough time in a day for us to perform due diligence on everyone with whom we do business. At some point, we have to rely on perception: a gut feeling, a hunch. Though these are educated opinions in some cases, they are also informed by seemingly irrelevant details: the organization of a proposal from your plumber, the fact that your insurance agent's laptop wasn't charged, or the eye contact (or lack thereof) from your teen son who wants to borrow your car for the evening. None is a direct reflection of competency or intention; yet when we have little else to go on, these are the things that motivate us to act, trust, or go elsewhere.

THE CASE FOR EXCELLENCE

Steve Jobs, Dick Hardt, and Randy Pausch didn't give their first presentations on the worldwide stage. Neither did I, and neither did you. Our passion—that sense of burning within, the pursuit of excellence that drives us to put on a smile and give our best to a room of disaffected teenagers at "Bring a Parent to Work Day," for instance—is the requisite ingredient for the future stage. Every presentation matters because while we have seven seconds to create an impression in someone's mind, we spend our entire lives revising, amending, and building on that first impression. Just because you met your spouse rescuing him or her from a burning building doesn't mean you ride out the marriage in permanent adoration. In the same vein, a good or bad beginning doesn't determine the outcome of a presentation, either.

It's simply a chance to build on the momentum we create, which is why pursuing excellence early and often begets more excellence.

Though my parents never told me to strive for excellence, they taught me many other values. In fact, I can still hear my mother's voice saying, "Scott, liars never prosper," "Do unto others . . ." or, "Scott Brent Schwertly, don't run in the house!" However, there was never anything about excellence—because it was implied. The highest virtues, it seems, are often implicit in our interactions. We expect goodness but rarely request it in written contracts. We want respect but command it with actions rather than demand it in words. Yet by the time many of us reach adulthood, we have learned to apply our most virtuous efforts in compartmental fashion, rather than in every facet of our life. We play hard for a quarter, but not the whole game.

Excellence is a function of sustained effort and direction. In a sense, it comes naturally: As kids, most of us gave 110 percent to something. For some of us, it was calculus; for others, it was Pac-Man. Thus, in another sense, it doesn't come naturally at all. We either develop a habit of pursuing excellence across the board, or we learn to apply ourselves based on individual circumstances. We attain results wherever we devote our time and resources; this is the rule that governs effort. A sustained effort in the field of fantasy football will generate a meteoric rise to the top of one's league. Over several seasons, I've watched individuals build fantasy dynasties around their skilled but fantasy leadership. Results follow excellence, no matter where it is applied.

Aristotle said we live most happily when we live most excellently. Accomplishment is intrinsically rewarding; we become happy when we apply ourselves. There is wildness to happiness, a sort of unchained revelry in the natural will not just to survive, but to flourish. When we engage with our ambitions and act with determination, we enjoy far more than just a comfortable lifestyle and financial security. We experience primal fulfillment—the sense that, between living and dying, we have chosen to live, and live well.

The ability to master PowerPoint depends on your primal fulfillment. The tools of the trade—props, projectors, laptops, and so on—are inanimate extensions of you. You wield them. You decide their function and how they serve your purpose. There is a disconnection between the service and the use of these tools, though. Unless, like me, you present on the topic of presenting, the tools of presenting are not directly related to your expertise. Because of this tangential relationship with PowerPoint and other presentation programs, passionately excellent businesspeople devote minuscule resources to their presentations—not realizing that an audience unfamiliar with their long pedigrees of excellence may well judge them on slide aesthetics, stuttering, and whether a hairstyle looks "intelligent."

We live most happily when we live most excellently: The more excellence we chase, the more happiness we can expect. Like Pac-Man prodigies turned businesspeople, most presenters put 110 percent effort into occupational excellence and far less effort into managing the perception of that excellence.

Using presentations to advance your happiness starts by redefining excellence. The aforementioned businesspeople fail to expend maximum efforts in their presentations because they don't see how perception and reality are connected. Simply put, presentations aren't important to them. They emphasize capability without thinking critically about whether or not they are producing an impression of capability in their audiences' minds. Yes, you will always have to support what is stated in a presentation; however, the opportunity to do so comes after the deal is made, not before. The deal is made on promises, not on actions. If you don't apply excellence to your presentations, you have essentially built a boat from the top down, worrying about winds and currents before thinking about whether the vessel will even float.

I have a unique privilege as an author: the simple fact that you have picked up this book means you are in the upper quartile of business professionals today, and rarely does one have the opportunity to speak intimately to such an elite group. You are improving yourself in areas outside of your expertise and applying excellence across the board. Just as my mother never explicitly told me to be excellent—but rather, emphasized the individual components of what comprised excellent living—so, too, do we need to refocus our efforts on the elements. We think of excellence in terms of action; it's time to think of excellence in terms of perception, too.

A LESSON FROM MR. RON BURGUNDY

In the 2004 film *Anchorman*, protagonist Ron Burgundy (played by Will Ferrell) has a central message to communicate to a beautiful woman, Veronica Corningstone (played by Christina Applegate): "I don't know how to put this, but I'm kind of a big

PRESENTATIONS ARE NOT A

FORMALITY;

THEY ARE THE

living
representation

OF

EVERYTHING

INVOLVED WITH BEING

YOU.

deal." The irony of the situation is that this is a true statement. Burgundy is San Diego's top newsman—a "god walking amongst mere mortals"—and he wields that authority with a sense of entitlement reminiscent of many businesspeople today. He doesn't realize that as someone new to San Diego, Corningstone cannot rely upon anything other than his presentation of the fact to decide whether or not she agrees. He is shaken by her ignorance of his reputation, unsure how to catch her up to speed, and ultimately arrogant and tongue-tied at the same time. She decides, for obvious reasons, that Ron Burgundy is not a big deal, regardless of the facts.

Nowadays many experts are running around like Ron Burgundy, assuming audiences understand their pedigree—indeed, that the audience knows they are a "big deal." So do something different by bringing a fresh approach to your expertise. Apply excellence across the board, and put an emphasis on proving yourself to an audience that doesn't know you—or one that could stand to be reminded. Learning how to quickly paint a picture of authority in listeners' minds is the difference between being a big deal and being a big deal *to them*. Burgundy's sin was not his ego or his factuality; it was failing to consider Corningstone's perspective and paint a picture of who he was in a way that resonated with her.

Presentations are not a formality; they are the living representation of everything that is involved with being you. Having the power to plan, create, prepare, and execute a presentation means having the power to own your message. Most people throw this power away. Embracing and using it will propel you in any direction of your choosing.

Chapter 3

Omniscient View

Let's establish something: Just because the Presentation Revolution is fomenting throughout the world, you don't have to hunker over your laptop and projector in fear that wild-eyed hooligans are going to throw Molotov cocktails on stage and loot your setup. Audiences are not upending conference tables or burning huge piles of complimentary hotel notepads. Physical danger is not imminent.

But every revolution makes someone mortally terrified or, at least, mildly uncomfortable. However, the Presentation Revolution has moved beyond discomfort. Several years ago it was making the old guard feel as though they'd been on a one-hour road trip; now, it's post-sugar, toddler-rage frightening. It will not be stopped; it will not be ignored; it will eat its cupcake and yours, too.

If the old guard (for example, individuals clinging to bullet-pointed PowerPoint presentations in the same way that a skeleton in the desert might still clutch a phony tonic purchased to guard against thirst) is not in danger of physical harm, what exactly should they fear? Oblivion is the fearsome wound most notably inflicted by the revolutionaries. Handed out like Depends at a bingo marathon, these energetic storytellers are taking their ideas, brands, and products to the world; they see need, and they see opportunity. The damage to the old guard is far worse than destruction; it is exclusion.

As *New York Times* columnist and author Thomas Friedman has illustrated, the world is now flat. Everyone is equal; opportunity abounds. You may have 40 years of experience in commercial trucking, but a small upstart working out of a two-bedroom home can win your best client if you let it out-present you. The best presenters are selling nothing less than unconditional love and acceptance. That is exactly how it feels to participate in a fantastic presentation.

Joining the revolution isn't a decision to enlist in anything. There are no forms, no dues, no initiations or minimum hours. Joining the revolution occurs the moment you make a decision to honor the process.

You won't believe in the revolution after a near-death experience; you won't wake up in the middle of the night with a presentation epiphany. The decision to join is far more calculated, and far simpler, than we might think. You don't *do* anything. So what is happening?

An opportunity comes along that you cannot lose—whether for ego, bank account, or a job. A magical transformation occurs in your mind, and the presentation becomes vastly important. Every transformation I've seen has come out of a similar, "I or my lifestyle will cease to exist," sort of bind. Thus, raising your expectations for excellence will make you a revolutionary faster;

JOINING THE
REVOLUTION
OCCURS THE MOMENT
YOU MAKE A
decision
TO
HONOR
THE
PROCESS.

lowering your expectations will delay it. Simply put: We think about presentations in a new light when it's lights out if we don't.

The revolution has no hub. There is no central office or communications department. The revolution's message exists solely in the hearts and minds of the individuals pressing forward, putting in the hours, and getting outside any boxes that make them feel a little too similar to the competition. It's your revolution, and it's mine.

This is a key realization because, as soon as our zeal motivates the pointer finger to perform the regrettable double-click on the PowerPoint icon, we want rules, hierarchies, and formulas. It's akin to the sudden awareness that peeling potatoes is actually a vital part of winning wars. Glory receives 99 percent of the press and 1 percent of our energy. The rest is setup and teardown.

When I ask you to join the revolution, I'm not asking for a fundamental shift in how you do business. Your success up to this point is predicated on *your* methods and *your* expertise. I'm simply asking you to raise your expectations. If you've been living as though there isn't much to gain from a great presentation, just imagine where you can go from here.

Without a single unified ideology directing the revolution, what, exactly, are we shooting for? Arming incompetent fools with tactics to swindle the masses hardly sounds like a great idea; it's like giving Segway scooters to rodeo clowns. How long will it take for us to arrive at the conclusion that agitated bulls and frivolous bipeds don't mix, regardless of the available technology?

Revolutionizing the presentation is essentially revolutionizing business; the scope is larger, which makes unifying theories irrelevant and binding. Presentations are conversations between the presenter and the audience about perception: How good are you at your job? How can I believe you? What about the other guys who say they are better? How should I decide?

Although one person speaks the entire time, these unspoken statements and questions are a real, living force in the room. Your ability to anticipate and answer the most important questions in the room—the ones that aren't asked—is the key to delivering a knockout presentation. Sometimes, the most powerful question in the room is, "Why am I here?" Answering that one makes you a presentation god.

As the digital age advances, consumers are becoming more empowered and more educated. I can use Google to find 16 local retailers for tires, plus another 50 online resources with blogs educating me on size, tread, brand reviews, and gas-saving tire tips. Facebook is there to remind me that my buddy is in the business. And though we have unprecedented access to information, we still have that same old desire to connect over business. At the end of the day, no matter how much I learn about tires, I still have to buy them from a human being who has to put them on my car. We are all generalists in the digital age. We know enough to ask the right questions, but never enough to do it all ourselves.

The presentation is changing with the world. Educated audiences are better audiences: When you don't have to start with Topic

101, you have the opportunity to display your expertise by being interactive, more creative, and deeper. In the omniscient view—the broad, history-encompassing, 30,000-foot view—the Presentation Revolution is a subsidiary of the Communication Revolution. Next year's business legends will be the ones that fought it out in the lecture halls and auditoriums all across the globe, digging deep to find new ways to do one thing: Reach out and touch someone, no matter what the topic. They'll do so partly by exploiting the opportunities technology has opened, and mostly by ignoring technology and aiming at the unchanging principles of humanity.

In other words—*this is happening*. Today, everything is available, all the time. Business doesn't wait till tomorrow; if it doesn't come to you, it's because someone else grabbed it first. The question that remains is what, exactly, you and I plan to do about it.

EXPAND YOUR HORIZONS

We've changed our expectations. We know what we've got to lose. We've mourned the old days, when our clients did business with us because they knew our old Aunt Ethel. Now Aunt Ethel can only get us a horse in the race, with no guarantee that we'll win. It's time to expand our horizons, to let go of locality and think bigger. Small-town business is great, but when small-town values become a comfort zone that smothers dreams and creativity, we need to branch out. The Presentation Revolution isn't about slick psychological manipulation; it's about improvement, each and every day, so that the best ideas, the best values, and the best people achieve success.

If we're going to expand our horizons, we have to lighten up. Not too long ago, people woke up to a day of hard labor, scratching the dirt, breaking the stones, surviving against all odds. This was accurately called work.

Nowadays, we make delicate keyboard strokes on ergonomically curved keys. We move a mouse a little to the left, a smidge up, and gently click. At times, we rise and walk to the bathroom. What we type, what we click, what decisions we make . . . are the things we get paid for now.

I'm not belittling what we do for a living. However, we need to recognize that we live in an "idea economy," one in which we get paid for our thoughts. Robots do a growing amount of mindless tasks on our behalf everyday. We cannot outmuscle them; we can only be paid for what they cannot do. We must stop referring to this as "work," as though it compares with the ancestral life of toil. We can have fun. We can *enjoy* this.

Despite this fact, many presenters make their presentations feel strikingly similar to scratching in the dirt, as if they are channeling primitive man. I see people every day who launch their presentations with charts. They begin with the assumption that people know why they are present, perhaps because of an agenda that says, "Marketing Budget Proposal." Easy, right? Everyone is there to hear about the upcoming marketing budget.

Wrong. Faced with the choice between indecipherable charts and battling a saber-toothed tiger for the one rabbit left in a five-mile radius, they'd all choose the tiger. But they don't have a choice.

Everyone is there because they have to be. They tried to get out and couldn't. They will attempt to avoid doing whatever it is you want them to do unless it is one thing: fun.

Our job when presenting is to magically transform outwardly boring subject matter into inwardly fulfilling action. We want to get the board completely psyched about spending more money for more results or have an on-the-fence potential client feel loved, respected, and excited about the prospect of spending hard-earned money on something we have to offer.

Expanding horizons is about changing our perspective. If we can't find a compelling story in the information we're sharing, why bother to share it? If it doesn't somehow relate to some element of the human experience, why should your audience do anything other than play Pong on their smartphones until you're done prattling on?

We have to stop looking at audiences as mere receptacles for information and knowledge. The human mind is better than any machine at making decisions and choices, but it is far more finicky. Studies have shown that we learn best through stories. Do you know what a mnemonic device is? It is a one, two, or three word *story*: something that attaches meaning to data, something that touches the heart in order to stay in the mind. Attach your dull data to a compelling story and see if the audience doesn't (1) thank you for not devaluing their existence and (2) remember and apply the information more readily.

How expansive is this approach? Wouldn't you think that, by now, Hollywood would have covered every story imaginable? Yet the movies flow like the butter off Grandma's pancakes. We digest an incredible amount of information from stories but often fail to recognize it. Connect with the heart and you get the mind, but there's no such thing as connecting with the mind.

BE FLEXIBLE

I'll warn you that new software will come out, new technologies will be developed, and audiences will doubtlessly change. They'll laugh at different jokes and find pleasure in emerging trends. If you are reading this book to find a list of current presentation skills that you can ride all the way into retirement, I have some very bad news.

We are not looking at trends; we are looking at principles. What kinds of ideas and approaches have resonated with audiences for centuries? How does the brain learn? How do the ears listen? What makes a person feel and do something? Answering these questions will revolutionize the world by drawing ideas and the people that put them into practice together more tightly than ever before. If we learn the principles, we can easily adapt to the trends. It's the difference between giving a good presentation and becoming a presentation god. Permanence and longevity are the measuring sticks.

Perhaps nothing illustrates principles-based learning better than the *Tao Te Ching*, an ancient Chinese text written by Lao Tzu that has influenced Eastern philosophy and religion for centuries. Stemming from the belief that everything in the natural world reflects unchanging, universal truths, the *Tao Te Ching* asked rulers and common people alike to be observant students of the world around them.

In an obvious, yet poignant, observation, Lao Tzu notices that those objects that are inflexible tend to break: "Gentle and yielding is the principle of life/Thus an Army without flexibility never wins a battle." Some withstand more force than others, but the slight and bending reed survives high winds better than the tall and rigid tree.

The lesson here is obvious: Be flexible. Follow the principles of good business, good politics, and good living. Recognize that forming relationships, caring about others, and providing perspective are standards of living that also go very well in your presentation, no matter its design style. We are a technical society: when we see a problem, we try to fix it. Rarely do we look within to consider the values we represent, yet nothing could be more vital when trying to motivate a group of people to act.

I say this because someone is inevitably going to spend hours developing a story, agonizing over the design, and perfecting the delivery of their presentation—only to walk into the venue and discover that the projector bulb is out, or a child replaced a memory card with a crayon, or that the airline didn't deliver their lost luggage on time. Though that person isn't responsible for whatever catastrophe has befallen their presentation, it *will* be their fault: an audience will show up nonetheless, and a presentation must be given. If we learn the principles that allowed Abe Lincoln, without PowerPoint, to connect with Americans at Gettysburg, or that let Churchill, *sans* laser pointer, to connect with the embattled and broken English people, then we'll know exactly what to do when that time comes.

ICEMAN

Meet **Iceman**. He makes his victims melt and break in the face of the slightest hitch during a presentation. He turns cool composure into thin ice.

A person can rise to the top of a company by developing an energetic and hilarious presentation style. But life is always changing. What happens when that humorous individual has to deliver a eulogy? What about hunger and war? If your only aspiration is to sell magician capes until you're filthy rich, life will eventually show you that you're needed for far more. Presentations can certainly be hilarious, but they need to provide strength and love and hope, too. Aspire to be all things to all people. There's no shortage of need for the aforementioned qualities.

If all we learn is a few canned story ideas, two or three fonts, and a favorite arm gesture or facial expression, we'll fall faster than Icarus with wings on fire. Again, be flexible. Focus on the principles and apply the tools. The omniscient view—the view that doesn't change, that never settles—is expansive. That kind of perspective requires that you open your heart enough to touch another person and be humble enough to step out of your experience and into someone else's. The irony of humility is that it determines your level of success, which will come if you expand your horizons and begin to engage with your audience. Practice flexibility by remaining open to new ideas and, more importantly, trying them out. I promise that you'll experience the thrill of discomfort and that you'll see results.

Lao Tzu also said, "A man with outward courage dares to die/A man with inward courage dares to live." Start taking bold steps to revolutionize the way you communicate. Science is increasing life expectancy, but not by that much. We have a short while to live among each other. Isn't it time we started making the most of our words and actions?

Chapter 4

The Pantheon of Presentation Gods

I'm familiar with the cynical sports purists who live among us: the know-it-alls who walk around crushing competitive cheerleaders' dreams, emasculating Nascar drivers, and begrudging soccer players their shin guards while applauding the armor plating that ensconces modern football players. The sports they know are the ones that matter.

No sport has been victimized by such so-called "purist" exclusivity than presenting. Yes—presenting. The sheer volume of pit sweat involved in this activity justifies an automatic Olympic event; the hoisting of a speaker challenges the celebrations of any victory in history. If gymnastics' menagerie of confusion, referred to as the "floor," can be a sport, then we presenters certainly deserve a place, too. I'm not asking for prime time major network coverage here, just a berth on a non-double-digits ESPN network.

Though securing ESPN9 or better may be one of the final achievements of the Presentation Revolution, that doesn't mean we can slack off as if our 2012 Olympic hopes are ruined. In the previous chapter, we discussed the value of humility from the stage, a statement that needs to be qualified as follows: You want the audience to *think* you're humble. Your will to crush the competition (in this case, other speakers, presenters, or companies) represents the furious passion that makes presenting one of the most exciting new sports to watch since little Western kids started rolling old wagon wheels with sticks. (One need only imagine a decades-long entertainment drought to understand just how exciting that might have been.)

So why are we competing? And what are the rules? These questions are meaningless for presenters. A breed focused on excellence, professional presenters are trying to win even when nothing is being played. They pour their hearts out, training for hours on end to master the technical skills and build up the strength to deliver ideas with true, contagious enthusiasm. Like Ron Burgundy, they are "gods among mere mortals," sucking the marrow out of life with the ferocity of a wolverine. (It's far less frightening to witness in real life than I've made it sound here.)

So who are these people? Where is the list of the world's best, the most potent iterations of communications mastery today? Sadly—and this may be one of the principle reasons Presenting will not have a team at the 2012 Olympics—there isn't one. Believe me, I've looked.

I want a top 10 list of the world's best presenters as much as the next guy, but we don't work in quantifiable figures like goals, saves, home runs, and so on. We're talking heart-and-soul economics, making people feel things. A casual journey through

MEDIOGRE

The lovely **Mediogre**. He is always attempting to block the road to achievement by pushing people towards mediocrity.

a Washington, DC, newspaper is enough to show that sometimes we say we felt what we didn't, and other times that we didn't feel what we did. In other words, it's tough to quantify who's winning in the sport of presenting, even if it's easy to know whose great and who's not great.

You would think that you could take a listing of international leaders and statesmen, combine it with a current *Forbes Richest People in the World* list, and end up with a more or less accurate picture of those people in the world who are presenting well—at least in the sense that nearly every idea they have is implemented wholeheartedly by the people who hear them. However, you would be wrong.

Though some degree of wealth and power tend to follow a consistently solid presentation performance, they are not directly correlated. Influence and impact are more accurate depictions of the fruits of great presenting. Presentation skills are difficult to measure. Like the Supreme Court in less savory matters, we know it when we see it; just (please) don't ask us to define it.

What we *do* know is that there have been presentation feats achieved throughout recent history that clearly show a standard of excellence across the entire sport. Some of these presentations have "gone viral"—despite the fact that they were given decades before going viral was even possible. Others illustrate the unique, changeable nature of the sport and demonstrate how capitalizing on new technologies and tools can yield glorious results. Here are some of the best moments in recent presentation history:

STEVE JOBS' 1984 INTRODUCTION OF MACINTOSH

Before the meek but iconoclastic hipsters in your neighborhood began wearing bowties, Steve Jobs was donning them with confidence. In an age when bowties were in enough to be out, rather than so out that they were in, this was definitely a bold move.

Jobs pulled a Mac out of a sack as if he were a magician—a moment of levity and showmanship that basically guaranteed that his once-yearly public addresses would be count-on-it stock boosts for years to come. And it has nearly been so. Add the *Chariots of Fire* theme song and you'll find yourself wanting to buy a new Mac based on a solid presentation given decades ago by the preeminent presentation god of the modern age. Jobs continues to show the importance of tension and release, buildup and discovery—and yes, hype—every year since.

MALCOLM GLADWELL'S 2005 *BLINK* PRESENTATION

To find the Malcolm Gladwell equivalent in another sport, you'd have to imagine Spud Webb wearing his shoes on the wrong feet and then performing like Michael Jordan. In other words, Gladwell so diverged from accepted good form in this presentation that you just can't believe how good he really was. He spoke too fast, used no visual aids, and scorned the laser pointer entirely. Then, he completely enthralled the audience. One might assume that had he continued to let words pour out of his mouth, those watching would have forsaken homes, families, and appetites just to stay and listen.

Gladwell's strength is his authority and ability to tell stories. Few presenters are as confident off-script as he is. Thus, without anything but his mouth and his hands, he is able to weave his tales and create an intimate connection with a rapt audience. If any one presentation demonstrates the importance of knowing your material inside and out no matter how long it takes, this is it.

JESSE JACKSON'S 1984 *DAVID AND GOLIATH* SPEECH

Whatever your politics, you know who he is and what he stands for. Long before he was the *de facto* pundit of democratic politics, he was a presidential candidate delivering speeches with a flavor only preacher-politicians can muster. Jackson exhibits one of the secret weapons of presenting: making the old new again. Every listener had no doubt heard the David and Goliath story—in many cases, more times than could be counted. But Jackson put a unique twist on the story, likening the fatal stone to unregistered voters, and he put a dramatically sharp edge on his point by doing so. He may not have won the presidency, but you can still see networks soliciting his opinions almost every week 26 years later.

Jackson demonstrates the value of fresh perspective. Presenters often agonize over generating brand-new, innovative content without realizing that sometimes a deft twist on an old story will do the trick just fine.

LAWRENCE LESSIG'S 2002 *FREE CULTURE* PRESENTATION

Lessig's slide usage was (and is) revolutionary: visually stunning, concise, and laser-targeted. The slide method he perfected has since become known as the "Lessig Method." His synergistic interaction with the projector, and the slide decks it displays, is reminiscent of a 2010 Ph.D. graduate and his parents: inseparable and destined to be together forever.

Lessig doesn't believe because he speaks; he speaks because he believes. He wants you to buy open-source culture, take it home, treasure it for decades, and then pass it on to your children. Although he provides logic, he ultimately sidesteps the brain and goes straight for the heart. The emotional connection is formed early and is repeatedly reinforced throughout the duration of the performance. Few speakers demonstrate such infectious belief; even fewer transmit it to the audience.

LOU GEHRIG'S FAREWELL SPEECH

Man is mortal. We're naïve to take the stage as though we have the luxury of time. Treating a message as though we have decades to impart it to the world isn't strategy; it's wasted time. If it matters, we should act as if only a short amount of time is available to get it out.

Lou Gehrig wasn't facing the end of an era or a cerebral notion of time. He had been promised certain death. Just as he stood so calmly at the plate and delivered year after year, he faced the unknown with a stoic grace that could make barbed wire cry.

Influence can be attained light-heartedly and with humor. However, the more successful we become, the more strength, fortitude, and vision will be required of us. Gehrig probably didn't have the courage to face the end with strength when he was just a rookie. He grew into his own legend, rising to a level of respect so high that the fact that he was a star baseball player came to be secondary to his reputation as a man. His example reminds us that the longer we present, the more character is demanded of us. We can hitch a great ride on a single presentation with high design and jokes—but if we want to become great, we have to be personally extraordinary.

ABRAHAM LINCOLN, PRESENTATION COACH

If you're cowering in anticipation of yet another one of those Lincoln-did-it-reading-by-candlelight-so-why-can't-you-get-the-Nike-account talks so often given by bosses, you can relax. Though I advocate the pursuit of excellence in all areas, I realize that encouraging people to shoot for Lincolnesque historical significance will make us more likely to end up paralyzed in our closets, sucking our thumbs rather than standing on stage with confidence. I'm not saying there are limits to your greatness; it's just best not to compare yourself with Lincoln in a competitive manner. It's not that he was a better person than any of us. Well, he was sort of.

How surprising! We have lessons to learn from our nation's most lauded public speaker and arguably most important president. During times of war we venerate Washington, but this year would have been Lincoln's 200th birthday if people lived that long. Thus, he's on our minds. Something of our current president, Barack Obama, calls to mind the echoing orations of Lincoln as well. They share a command of the inspirational, a penchant for cadence and word choice that seems to grip an audience's ears, and a height advantage over most of their peers. Obama scorns the top hat—evidently a decision that may ultimately be the deciding difference between the two men. Time will tell.

Modern media coverage makes it possible for us to view and review speeches, isolating with sterile precision the intonations, facial gestures, and enunciations that make or break good communication. We can record a voice and digitally compare it with the cadence of another until we grasp what it is that is so aurally arresting about the sound. Yet for all our science, at the end of the day, there is one plain and simple reality: Either we join the speaker's plea, or we don't. No amount of technical tweaking can trump the movements of the heart.

Thus, 200 years after his birth—with no video, no recordings, and few pictures—we are still able to reconstruct the singular talents of an incredible president. By distilling them down to the actionable steps we all can take, we can perhaps elevate ourselves on his example, even if we cannot equal his unparalleled strength. The following are some of the ultimate presentation god's best-known tactics.

Abe the Beanstalk

Of course, from a physical standpoint, Lincoln stood out in a way that only tall people can—that is, by being tall. But he didn't rely solely on this natural endowment to deliver the full effect of his stature: he added a top hat. He had height, so he underlined it 20 times and drew arrows all around it. He was an outsider, a country boy of sorts, and he combined this reputation with his physical originality to suggest that he was a solid, immovable force. In the end, his character and bearing backed up every perceptual promise several times over.

WE CAN'T ALL BE

TALLER

than everyone in a room,

BUT THE LESSON TO BE
LEARNED FROM LINCOLN

isn't
"BE TALL";

IT IS

"accentuate your
STRENGTHS."

We can't all be taller than everyone in a room, but the lesson to be learned from Lincoln isn't "be tall"; it is "accentuate your strengths." Think of Woody Allen's hyper-nerd glasses: they force us to see him as the character he so often is. What about Jim Cramer? His shtick is the up-all-night frenzied stock trader, and his outfit—coat off, suspenders, tie on but loosened, sleeves rolled up—makes you feel like he's talking to you in the 11th hour of the best or worst day in history. Granted, the standard for entertainers is different than for the average presenter, but everyone has an opportunity to use appearance to help deliver the message. Is your style quirky and offbeat? Try an outfit that's just a little step apart from the norm, with a bowtie or silly cufflinks. Are you a driver, using build-up and energy to ram your point home? Trademark powerful dress, coordinate ties with your slide deck, and make the presentation a train that people must board before you run them over.

Every presentation god follows Lincoln's example here. To be the best, we must be magnetic and commanding. Lincoln was a farm boy. I can promise you he did not feel magnetic when he began to raise his ambitions. He took stock of his assets, from physical to mental to ideological, and turned every aspect up as loud as it would go. It's a good thing he did, too: Otherwise, can you imagine what the import taxes for sending this book from New York to Georgia would be?

Stutter Suppression

Presenting puts you up on a pedestal; it produces a feeling in most people akin to reliving, in slow motion, the most humiliating moment of adolescence. In our personal terror, we often forget that this pedestal simultaneously engenders feelings of admiration, envy, and submission in the audience, essentially forming an impenetrable barrier against embarrassment on our behalf. Until we stutter 43 times between the words, "Good afternoon," that is. The wall can come down, but it is there.

For all we know, Abe Lincoln may have spent 10 minutes behind an oak tree puking his guts out before delivering the Gettysburg Address. But from the moment he opened his mouth, he proceeded as if he was ordained by God Almighty to save the nation.

You need not be bold, courageous, or decisive in the face of challenges and deadlines, or possess any other admirable quality to be a stellar presenter. You may find it difficult to be invited on stage without these qualities, but once there, you only have to convey those qualities. For the other 23 hours of every day spent off stage, you can cry into pillows, ask for your mother, and drink out of bottles and Sippy-cups. When you step on stage, though, it's time to channel Lincoln: Think calm and composed. Imagine that the entire universe is aligned to support your every effort. Audiences know far less about us than we think. Take solace in that fact—and get that bottle out of your mouth!

Preparation Proclamation

Even if you can stand flat-footed, stare directly into the eyes of a giraffe, and ask, "How much wood would a woodchuck chuck if a woodchuck could chuck wood?" without stuttering while watching someone take the thing you love the most—say, a childhood blanket—and tear it in two, you are not automatically walking among gods. That is, physical presence and cool delivery in the face of enormous pressure don't make you a star. When it comes down to it, audiences do two things: watch and listen. Because of this, you'll need to actually say something meaningful at some point. This is one of those pesky little truths about public speaking.

Abraham Lincoln agonized over his content. His ideas were born out of genuine reflection during long, long walks. He scribbled his nebulous thoughts on scrap pieces of paper, contemplated, wrote, and revised them. His raised his content with meticulous deliberation out of the hatchery of his mind. By the time he gave a speech, the ideas were fully formed, distilled from raw ingredients into potently influential monologues.

True preparation goes beyond memorization. It is the pursuit of such thorough familiarity with every facet of your content that you go far beyond merely delivering a message; you personally represent it with your heart, mind, and body.

I WANT TO JOIN THE PANTHEON. WHERE DO I SIGN?

Discuss the legends in any field for long enough, and a sinking feeling can settle in. So often the advice seems to be along the lines of, "Go forth, and be awesome—more awesome, in fact, than you have ever been." Clearly, such advice treats success as if it were a red pill and failure a blue pill. Beyond a few comedians whose slacker personas actually serve them better than ambition, I think we'd all be downing the reds, given the choice.

A survey of the greats—Jobs, Gladwell, Lessig, and so on—might make the art of the presentation seem unattainable. None of the greats are genetically predisposed to captivate audiences, though. The best in every field do all the right things so naturally that we forget how much practice it took for them to get there. Roger Federer was training three times a day as early as age six; Tiger Woods, it seems, was handed a putter shortly after the umbilical cord was cut. Superiority is laid one brick at a time, day by day.

We can either be daunted by these geniuses' commitment, or we can be greatly encouraged by realizing that being the best depends almost entirely on the things that we do all day. It's a result of the actions and behaviors over which we have direct, moment-to-moment control. Joining the pantheon of presentation gods will entail both your time and commitment. Like any sport, it will require coaching, both for directing your efforts and for constant feedback. In the following chapters I'll detail a specific plan for enhancing every area of your presentation: content, design, and delivery. But my schedule simply won't permit me to travel to your home, sit on your couch, and watch you practice—even if you do keep your refrigerator well stocked with Blue Moon beer. Ultimately, you are going to need a partner—a coworker, spouse, or friend—who can give you honest feedback while you train. I can't tell you how many times my wife has pointed out a nervous tic of mine that I had no idea I was doing. A second pair of eyes will keep you from reinforcing bad habits along the way.

Three is a magic number. Bridges are built with triangle trusses; stools with three legs are strongest. My mother gave me three seconds to listen and obey. How did she know two seconds wasn't long enough and that four was far too long? It seems we have a natural, almost innate understanding of the power of threes. The same power applies to presentations. To join the pantheon, you'll need to master three key areas.

Content

If we're really going to boil it down, this is the whole enchilada. Without content, your presentation is either an art show or a mime performance; the former won't advance your cause, the latter is so unpopular it's relegated to city parks and sidewalks.

You must nail down your content before doing anything else. Always establish your expertise early on, as part of the flow of your presentation, or you'll be astonished at how quickly people disregard every word you say. A plumber and a heart surgeon can give the exact same speech about modern advancements in bathroom plumbing, and even though both individuals deal in pipes, the audience will only care about what the plumber has to say. When the speech is about bypass surgery, guess whom we want to hear from? Facts, figures, and information only matter if the person stating them has the perceived authority to do so.

In almost every circumstance, if you've been asked to speak, you're probably an expert. Your familiarity with the subject matter is both your greatest asset and your greatest weakness. Your audience is an audience because they don't know as much as you do about a particular topic; otherwise, they wouldn't show up or would be giving the presentation themselves. Identifying with the audience and understanding the extent of their knowledge is vital to making your content novel, interesting, and accessible. Going over (or under) their heads is, essentially, wasting their time. Finding the sweet spot is the key to delivering top-notch content.

Design

To the innovative computer scientist, a projector screen of binary code looks like *See Spot Run*. To an audience, it looks like a perverse game of Brain Twister in which the brain's lobes get so knotted that they collapse. In this Twister horror, there is no laughter at the end and no newly formed crushes among childhood friends. There is only pain and agony.

Design makes you make sense. If we just wanted the facts, we'd buy a few textbooks in the field and start reading. We've called you in to distill your knowledge to us simply and concisely—and nothing is more concise than imagery. A picture can be worth a thousand words, but not if that picture is a garbled nest of charts designed in Microsoft Paint. Therefore, I have to clarify: *Good* design makes you make sense. Bad design does more for the dismemberment of your reputation than forgetting to wear pants on the big day.

Presenters either fear design or don't respect it. Our culture tends to keep art and business separate—a trend that, combined with the level of technical proficiency necessary to achieve good design, can lead a lot of public speakers to rely on comfortable but unstylish bullet points and clip art. This approach is roughly as sexy as a snoring octogenarian in a recliner with his or her teeth percolating in seltzer water nearby. You may revere the speaker's wisdom, but you're still averting your eyes.

Delivery

Perhaps the greatest example of good delivery is found during our first introduction to the Wizard of Oz (the character, not the movie). He is terribly frightening, an imposing figure that easily convinces Dorothy and her cohort to do exactly as he wishes—to go away.

The worst example is also the Wizard of Oz, during his second appearance. He is careless, revealed, and then controlled by his audience. Our onstage performance—facial expressions, tone, nonverbal cues—can either serve as the finishing touch on our master plan or our inescapable demise. Delivery is a double-edged sword for many people; it requires a fervent and committed effort to perfect while becoming natural and easy with practice. Putting in the hours early on will pay great dividends for any speaker looking to join the pantheon.

GETTING DOWN TO BUSINESS

The stage is set. The lights are low. The *Jock Jams* introduction music is thumping. By the time you finish this book, you'll be completely equipped to deliver Wizard of Oz 1.0 presentations. You'll control your audience as though they were puppets, opening their wallets for your charity or thoroughly convincing them that a pillow that vibrates in the morning is just the alarm clock that their stores need. Whatever you set out to accomplish, the presentation tactics we're about to cover will put the tools of the gods at your disposal. My only request is that you use your newfound powers for good, not evil.

Raise your sights. Put on your seatbelt. Put the Sippy-cup down and take up a beer stein or, better yet, a coffee mug. We're adults here. It's time to get to work. The Presentation Revolution is alive and well; there are presentations to build, design, and deliver—presentations that dominate. I'll see you on the other side!

Chapter 5

Don't Ruin Their Day!

Amid the countless variables that occupy your thoughts in the weeks leading up to a presentation—hairstyles, clothing, what to eat for breakfast, the subject matter—you can be certain of two things. And no, they're not death and taxes. Cryogenics and modern medicine have advanced to the point that humankind can at least begin to delude itself with the notion of immortality, even if it is at the expense of a freezer-burned nose and, if you're still paying taxes, maybe it's time to start sending Uncle Sam postcards from the Caribbean.

No, the certainties in the presentation world are simple: (1) your presentation is vital to the advancement of your career, your business, and/or humanity; and (2) your audience would rather you show up with an inflatable ball pit than a projector and laser pointer. Your human audience is like a car with golf cart tires on one side and monster truck tires on the other: It's going to take a significant steering effort to keep it on the road.

These two realities arm the presenter with a unique capability: to completely ruin hundreds, even thousands of days, all at once. An audience arrives for a presentation with a certain amount of knowledge; if you spend an hour repeating that knowledge to them, you've effectively wasted their time. They come to you with a desire to learn something; give them unorganized and indecipherable information and you've ruined their day. They show up at the expense of other items on to-do lists that sprawl beyond the confines of their cubicles; fill your presentation with unrelated stories and jokes and you're sure to watch as they foam at the mouth, chain the dais to the nearest unattended vehicle, ignite said dais, and drive around the venue seven times until the rubble closely resembles your newly amended reputation.

While not every gathering of people is a guaranteed riot, the presenter should always approach content as though rioting is a possible outcome. This doesn't mean you need to start scouring Craigslist for Kevlar vests; rather, give thoughtful consideration to how you spend your audience's time. While presentations are responsible for the most significant movements in human history—they're given before deciding battles; they ignite reforms and revolutions; they bring the ShamWow to a desperate public—we find very few individuals counting the days to the next one. Maybe just myself, even.

What your mother told you all those years ago is still true: If you want to be respected, you have to give respect. Your number one job as a presenter is to respect the audience by preparing a clear, concise, informative, and efficient presentation. Remember: You have seven seconds from the time you take the stage before they begin making sweeping judgments about you. Without solid preparation and a clearly outlined game plan, it is inconceivable that you will convey respect in those seven seconds. And disrespect is a very hard first impression to overcome.

WHAT YOUR *mother* TOLD YOU ALL THOSE YEARS IS **TRUE:**

IF YOU WANT TO BE **respected,** YOU HAVE TO **give respect.**

For those with phobias of agitated crowds, riot gear improvised from office equipment, or bodily harm, there are a few easy-to-implement steps that you can take to make their time worthwhile. Following a standard protocol in the weeks leading up to your presentation will help you ensure that you are always on the side of the revolutionaries and never against them. By clarifying your objective(s), brainstorming and developing a theme, and thoroughly outlining your content, you can avoid ruining days and, instead, start getting things done.

CLARIFY YOUR OBJECTIVE

The cardinal sin of presenting is failing to address the presentation's objective or objectives. You would think that this is nearly impossible; after all, the speaker has received a topic that is listed on meeting schedules and agendas. But because so much of the content we're presenting these days is so vast, so complicated, or in such gray areas, presenters often get lost in their own labyrinthine heads. I've seen it before: A presenter ends up spending 45 minutes of an hour-long time slot discussing the science behind a new medical tool when all the audience wants to know is the long-term financial cost. Sure, both topics are connected to the device in question, but only one gives the audience exactly what they need and nothing more.

A good starting point for clarifying your objective is to write a single mission statement for your presentation. Contact a representative from the audience or the organization that's requested the presentation, and read this mission statement to them. Ask them if it is (1) exactly what they want to learn, discuss, and so on, or (2) *not* exactly what they want to learn, discuss, and so on. You've gone to great lengths to avoid being a career waiter or waitress, but like waiting tables, these presentations are a service, not a product. Your job is to find out what the audience needs and give it to them. And also like waiting tables, the faster and more fun you make it, the better. People will ask to sit in your section again and again.

Now that you've clearly identified exactly what your presentation is supposed to accomplish, write it everywhere: on Post-it notes, on whiteboards, on Word documents, and on anything else associated with the engagement. The next steps—brainstorming and outlining—must serve this mission. You must keep it forefront in your mind at all times or else you will be amazed at how easily a tangled web of case studies, anecdotes, charts, and graphs can form.

BRAINSTORMING AND DEVELOPING A THEME

This is where you get to play James Carville or Mary Matalin, depending on your politics. You know exactly what you want to communicate—for illustration purposes, we'll pretend that they desperately want to know if you are awesome—and now it's time to pave a clear road to the logical conclusion that because of X, Y, and Z, you are exactly that. We have to use our heads here, because there is a distinct difference in whether the audience wants to know *why* you are awesome and *if* you are awesome. *Why* suggests that while they suspect you are awesome, they want quantitative evidence for this assertion—you run the 100m dash in such and such time, your hair smells like coconut and roses, you yodeled in Switzerland for P.E. credits in college, and so on. *If*, on the other hand, suggests that they have doubts about your awesomeness—they saw a YouTube video of you dancing at a bar several weeks ago and now seriously question whether you are capable of coaching their pre-K dance team.

Brainstorming must be a comprehensive process wherein nuance is the name of the game: We're trying to find a balanced, effective message for a specific demographic and a specific objective. Convincing the board you're the guy who can cut distribution costs by 33 percent requires an understanding of what matters most to a board member; convincing the hardworking folks down in the warehouse to work more efficiently, cap salary increases, and eliminate unnecessary positions will take a different approach. Although we're cutting distribution costs by 33 percent regardless, only one group is predisposed to like it.

The pitfalls should be obvious. In the latter scenario—trying to encourage a group of warehouse workers to do more for less—you clearly don't want images of suit-wearing businessmen, rising stock prices and profits, and so on. Here, we'll focus on pride in hard work, job security, and the correlation between company contributions to 401(k)s and company efficiency. With any luck, a strong correlation exists.

No matter whom you're speaking to, you will rarely be personally representative of your target demographic. Board members don't present to each other; they listen and discuss together. Warehouse workers are the same. Each party communicates with the other, something that requires a strong effort in taking different perspectives. Not doing so guarantees that first, second, and third ideas will likely end up being tossed in the trash. If you cut out brainstorming, you may walk into your speaking engagement holding a very, very hot potato with no one to whom you can toss it.

Beyond the primary pitfall of poor brainstorming, there is a second hazard: audience fatigue. Imagine how often groups of warehouse workers are visited by management types and implored to work harder, more efficiently, and with little to no hope of pay raises. Don't you think managers have used up every analogy that can be thought up during a 10-minute potty break?

Unless you are Don Draper, the consummate ad man of AMC's *Mad Men* (and someone who *still* takes a profound amount of time to brainstorm), the first ideas that come to your head are most likely the easiest, most conventional, and most boring ideas you will have. The human mind works like this: We're creatures born to survive, which means that we opt to conserve energy whenever possible. Your brain will sabotage your efforts at brilliance by attempting to find the easiest, most accessible solutions for any problem it is faced with. Conserving resources has been a recipe for survival for as long as organic life forms have existed; you and I are no different.

A great way to hurdle this unfortunate mental obstacle is to begin every brainstorming session thinking about what *not* to do. Work with partners to determine what is cliché, what is expected, what has been heard over and over and over again. Record these ideas and you'll begin to find the empty space—the place where you have an opportunity to approach the topic from a fresh

NARCO-LEPTO

Narcolepto loves crushing audiences
with a suffocating blanket of 'zzz's

angle, introduce a new idea, or catch your audience offguard. Accomplishing a sense of originality is like putting a massive sail on the canoe of your presentation: It will take you further than even your hardest work.

Try to avoid creating a static and monotonous environment during the brainstorming phase. Our brains are scripted: We think in certain ways in certain scenarios. While breaking out of these predetermined scripts is crucial to getting novel material, you'll never achieve this by locking the same five people in a conference room day after day. Mix it up: Work both individually and in groups. Break off in pairs; convene for collective discussion. When things get stagnant, head to a coffee shop, go for a walk—just do *something* different. Contrary to popular belief, creativity is both culture and practice; it is not a gift that some people just have and others don't. Breaking away from the script is as simple as keeping your brain on its toes, and that means changing environments, having new interactions, and maintaining continued engagement.

Eventually, you and your team arrive at a decisive theme that runs through the entire presentation. This theme—which is usually an analogy or metaphor of some sort—acts as a grounding wire for an audience trying to keep up with your expertise. They may not understand cloud computing, but they do understand the water stations at marathons: Doesn't it make more sense to get your water from the station nearest to you, rather than the one back at mile six? Doesn't it make more sense to keep it constantly available on an as-needed basis by providing a host of easily accessible stations, rather than wheeling a water cart for 26.2 miles? When the technical jargon gets confusing, the audience can always compare what you are saying to something comfortable and familiar—as long as you provide a continuous theme.

And please, do make sure it is continuous. Theme hopping may sound like something college graduates should do for a year before entering the workforce for the remainder of their lives, but in reality, this tactic is frustrating and really not any better than having no theme at all. Cloud computing is either lightweight, easily accessible refreshment during a marathon, or it is a pond of ever-present lily pads providing frogs with constant safety as they flee a hungry largemouth bass (clearly representing the threat of data overload on terrestrial servers, not to mention the operating costs). Make it both, and you'll have an audience picturing frogs running marathons while trying to figure out why a marathon runner would be afraid of a largemouth bass.

You'll notice that whatever we say cloud computing is, we do not say that it is like clouds—because seven of our competitors have already delivered this white and fluffy angle. Taking the same approach is likely to make the audience's choices foggy, and we want the choices clear as the blue sky because we want to be chosen. Take the extra couple of days to really dig down deep and come up with a truly unique approach. He who gives an ingenious presentation is himself ingenious—and we all prefer to work with ingenious people.

Now that you've brainstormed and developed your theme, it's time to lock it down. We're going to make the switch from

MacGyver to Matlock—from creative to pragmatic—so that our presentation contains both the spark of originality and the raw power of sound logic. Think of your presentation as the annoying memos about dress code violations in the office and presentation success as landing those memos in a trashcan as far across the office as possible (for dramatic effect). Clarifying objectives and thoroughly developing themes are wadding up the memo; outlining the presentation is like the toss. Skip the first two steps, and no one knows where the flat sheet is going. Skip the last step, and you've got a beautifully crumpled, annoying memo still sitting on your desk. Practice enough and you'll fill that trashcan up with so many annoying memos they'll put you right in the corner office (provided you clean up your attire, that is).

OUTLINE YOUR CONTENT

When it's time to outline your content, you must shut your creative side out of the room. If it tries to get in, have a bouncer punch it in the stomach. The creative work is done; now it's time to incorporate this artistic material into a factual, well-researched body of information so that the audience can learn something, not just be entertained.

Your outline is your court case. We're not thinking out of the box anymore; we're thinking if/then, cause and effect, logic and reason. I'm not devaluing creativity; after all, we've spent days on the creative process. But we have to put a serious face on at some point. If you're not going to provide the aforementioned inflatable ball pit, you'd better provide something meaningful. Really, it's one or the other.

Outlines need structure to balance the tangential mind.
Human beings are capable of connecting thousands of bits of
information to one idea (which is overwhelming) and of finding
great importance in other ideas despite a lack of supporting
information (which is vexing). I work in groups of threes so that
my presentations have balance. There are three reasons what I'm
saying is true; there are three illustrations for each reason; and
there are three things I want you to do, now that you understand.

If I can't come up with more than two reasons, illustrations, or
actions, I know that I don't have a complete thought and it's back
to brainstorming on that one. If I can't narrow it down to three
key points in any given area, then I might not understand my own
content. Since that will come through during the presentation, it's
back to the drawing board again. (Note: If you have been asked
by a board member to present on the four guiding principles
of the company, please do not engage in an argument about
distilling those principles down to a tidy three. Just deal with it.)

From a bird's eye view, we're talking about the classic thesis paper
format we learned in high school: introduction, thesis statement
(objective), supporting paragraphs, and a conclusion that
demonstrates the implications of the information. Don't worry if
this sounds elementary; I actually imagine that a 10-year-old is in
the back of every room I speak to. My mission when on stage is not
to stun the audience with illustrious vocabulary and capacity for
arcane bits of knowledge. It is to efficiently transmit a valuable
concept or idea to their heads with as little interference as possible.
If a 10-year-old can't follow me, then an adult whose attention
is split between his or her BlackBerry and my voice can't, either. I

PARTY FAVOR

Party Favor's tongue is like a cheap blow toy that unfurls, flaps incessantly and makes awful noises. He slays audiences with excessive and unnecessary talking.

work hard to be entertaining so that the smartphones don't come out, but have you played with these things? They're ridiculously addictive, so keep the content simple.

A study of the accessibility of three computer industry magnates—Steve Jobs, Bill Gates, and Michael Dell—illustrates this point beautifully. Jobs' presentations have been pegged at a fifth grade difficulty level—slightly older than my imaginary 10-year-old. Gates speaks at a ninth grade level, Dell at an eleventh grade level. Jobs' Apple Corporation is taking over the world, Microsoft is progressing at a slightly lesser speed, and Dell certainly trails in third place. If we have big dreams, we need large groups of people—clients, consumers, coworkers, or citizens—to help us. The larger these groups, the more important it is that we keep our content simple and direct. With luck, the Presentation Revolution will have us all speaking on an infantile level one day, with flashing lights and baby talk. Just imagine what we can accomplish then!

Every portion of your outline—introduction, thesis, supporting points, and conclusion—serves a master: the clearly identified objective(s) we started with. With that in mind, here is how to use each section:

1. **Introduction.** A brief moment of connection or levity, the introduction allows you to be a human being instead of a data-spewing machine. Establish the metaphor or analogy that you'll be using as a ground wire for the remainder of the presentation. Comfort the audience by explaining what you'll be doing for the next 45 minutes, hour, or however

long you have. Make it fun, make it snappy, but most of all, make it original and poignant. Your introduction should build to one irrefutable conclusion: that you will meet the objective for the day.

2. **Thesis.** This irrefutable conclusion is your thesis, and it uses the story from your introduction's theme to concisely establish that you have whatever the audience is looking for. A hotel chain is looking to save money with a new soap manufacturer; like SPAM, your soap is cheap, lasts forever, and contains less than 2 percent real meat. Perhaps during your brainstorming session you can come up with something more palatable. I'm not giving my best ideas away for free here.

3. **Supporting Points.** This is your opportunity to prove that you don't just travel all over the globe speaking in superlatives and hoping some poor corporation abhors due diligence and buys your soap. In your three supporting points, you will begin to establish the cold, hard facts that prove beyond a shadow of a doubt that you, your product, or your company do whatever it is you promise to do. You say your soap is cheap? How about a comparative analysis of cost between your product and the top competitors in the industry? (Note: these are *your* supporting points, not those of some independent third party. You have control over perspective; does the soap cost more but last even longer? Or maybe it doesn't last as long, but since most guests steal the soap, paying for longevity is tantamount to wasted money in the hospitality world. Truth is, indeed, relative now. Your supporting points help the audience know how to view the facts and figures.)

4. **Conclusion.** The average adult's short-term memory allows the storage of information (without practice) for a few seconds to about a minute or so. This is limited to seven pieces of information. Even if it were five minutes and 30 pieces of information, the ramifications of this mental iniquity are obvious for presenters: you've just handed a body of information to a group of adults who haven't been able to hold onto any seven pieces for longer than a minute or so (at best). If you don't find a way to recap everything you've discussed at the end, you may as well have done the entire presentation with your best impersonation of Charlie Brown's teacher.

Don't get bogged down when you're so close to the end. Recap your thesis and supporting points, keeping them neatly in the story you set up with the introduction. Don't worry about reviewing the details of your supporting points: while your audience may not be able to repeat verbatim the significant data points on each slide, they'll have a strong sense that you made a clear and logical argument. The conclusion is simply a brief review of what just happened: We gathered together because of this problem, I put the problem in terms you could understand, explained why I have the solution for your problem, and then provided proof of my solution to you. Here's how you get in touch with me and sign the contract that will make me partner.

We've just gone through a structure that will ensure that you consistently give targeted, relevant presentations that don't ruin any days. Through clarifying and brainstorming, content takes on fresh, original, and arresting qualities. Our outline makes the form serve the function, the art serve the objective.

So what now?

DRILL, BABY, DRILL

Now, you rehearse. Study the research; examine the case studies; practice, practice, practice. I never go on stage without eight dry runs under my belt—preferably more. You might think it sounds tedious, but I disagree: A 100-member audience attending an hour-long presentation is giving up 100 collective hours. The least I can do is spend eight hours over the course of several weeks tweaking, whittling, and honing my content. I'll clarify what is important and what can be cut. I'll communicate respect for their time. I'll feel absolutely and unstoppably confident when I take the stage. I will win, even if there isn't a competition.

Don't go through the trouble of clarifying, brainstorming, and outlining only to get on stage and give a tentative performance. Persuasion is about *perceived* authority; even if you say the exact same words with or without practice, I promise the *effect* will be greater with practice. Aim to appear as if your content is spilling off the top of your head, just the way you would speak with a family member or friend. And keep practicing until you reach that point.

SNAPSHOT OF A PRESENTATION GOD: BRUCE LEE

Nothing presents like a fist in the face. But even lacking that option, we can still learn a lot from the late martial arts master.

Bruce Lee wasn't just good at martial arts; he revolutionized them by creating a brand new style called *Jeet Kune Do*, thereby changing expectations about how the arts were learned. Here's what we can learn from Lee for that upcoming presentation.

Pragmatism

Being pragmatic mean having a basic understanding of priorities: If you want to deliver an authentic, original presentation, don't place exclusions on how that presentation comes into being. I see presenters every day who limit what they can and can't do on stage according to the assumptions they've made about themselves such as, "I'm not creative," "I'm not energetic," or "I'm not good with words." At the end of the day, just decide what's more important: what you "know" about yourself or giving a great presentation. We can choose to be whatever we need to be when we prioritize a goal over our own egos. Again, creativity isn't a gift; it's an attitude.

Espionage

Put the martini down because I don't mean pursuing your lifelong dream of living life on the razor's edge. Lee possessed the *spirit* of espionage in spades—a deeply held belief that learning was available everywhere. The casual observer would assume that a 5'7", 135-lb. martial artist couldn't learn much from the 6'3", 220-lb. heavyweight champion of the world Muhammad Ali. He did, though, despite their differences in frame and style. Lee ventured out of his niche frequently and was even reputed to be an ardent fan of professional wrestling. So take a cue from Lee and practice maintaining this level of heightened awareness. Themes, stories, illustrations, and tactics will come to you much more easily if you open your eyes to the world around you. Everything is fair game for inspiration.

Build a Brand

Bruce Lee constantly innovated. His competition focused on established techniques and perfecting existent strategies; Lee mastered them, then moved on. He lived and fought in his own realm, and his competition was often forced to assume a purely defensive posture in the face of such originality. Innovation inspires ownership, one of the most powerful forces in life and business. Top performers are accountable for themselves—a quality that's clearly magnetic. Don't settle for just finishing the presentation; set out to build a brand out of yourself and the expertise you possess. The ownership will add originality and accountability to everything you do and will greatly improve the quality of your content.

Open Your Heart

Lee turned the exclusive world of Kung Fu into an accessible international phenomenon. His films are engaging to nearly everyone, regardless of martial arts interest. His studios welcomed non-Chinese students, which at the time was an act of unprecedented integration. He encouraged and uplifted his co-stars on the set throughout his acting career, despite having every right to be aloof and egomaniacal (I think the ability to beat up everyone on earth at least explains, if not justifies, an ego).

So let me reiterate: Don't ruin your audience's day. Dynamic content may require a combination of strategy and innovation

STRATEGY
IS A
cognitive
EFFORT;

INNOVATION
IS A
movement
OF THE
HEART.

that forces you to change what you've been doing, but life is short. Shouldn't we embrace change at every turn? The strategy is as simple as putting the steps to great content in your calendar. Take time to clarify objectives; create a space for real, in-depth brainstorming and theme development. Make a detailed outline that serves as a roadmap for your message, and then practice like it's the last chance you'll ever have to speak. The energy that freewheeling creativity and disciplined preparation create is unmistakable. Your audience not only will appreciate your efforts but will be inclined to follow you.

The innovative mindset, however, will take more than just calendar entries. You'll have to connect your heart to your presentation's outcome, since nothing else alerts the mind like a heartfelt, earnest goal. Engross yourself in the opportunities your speaking engagements create, and you'll be surprised at what pops out at you during everyday life. Strategy is a cognitive effort; innovation is a movement of the heart. The revolutionaries are more than great speakers: They're connected to their message in a revolutionary way. How can you ratchet up the feeling and energy necessary to take your presentations to the next level?

Chapter 6

You Matter

Our age—the digital age—lets us quantify everything. We can measure almost every behavior with minuscule tools, allowing us to know the raw math and science behind more and more activity every day. In an increasingly empirical society, we have a tendency to over-rely on the substance of what we say and downplay the representative—in many cases, ourselves.

Yes, credibility depends in large part on the initial presence and veracity of real, meaningful data. Expertise requires a mastery of the most up-to-date information in a particular field. But when we talk about credibility in the presentation world, we don't mean whether or not the contents of your head justify your presence on stage. We're talking about whether the audience is inclined to believe anything that comes out of your mouth.

We can complain that this is unfair, that we shouldn't have to be a slave to audience perception, that people should make their judgments on the facts and not the apparent strength of the presenter. We can hem and haw about the post-physical world, where Steve Urkel and Conan the Barbarian have the same shot at getting the girl. Or, we can empathize with the audience for a change.

After all, what *do* they know about you? Perhaps they know you have a Ph.D. from a great school. Maybe they saw you arrive in a nice car, or maybe they read a short biography about you in the meeting agenda, or heard about you from a co-worker. But what do any of these so-called credentials mean to them? Regardless of your actual intelligence, pedigree, or achievements, the reality is that your audience has very few reasons to think anything about you, let alone trust you. Trust is an emotional commitment, not a rational decision.

This scenario can play into your favor, if you allow it to. The power of implied authority is strong, and speakers are suffused with this power at the outset of a presentation. You are physically elevated above the audience. You are the only person in the room facing a different direction; everyone is looking at you. You're dressed nicer than everyone else or, failing that, dressed more freely. Proving your credibility to the audience isn't going to require eyebrow tweezing, expensive suits, and various feats of strength. The psychological setting means you begin with a certain level of trust automatically. Unfortunately, the problem many speakers encounter is that they lose this trust shortly after opening their mouths.

This is your implied contract: The audience gives you the benefit of the doubt, and you in turn don't let them down. Of course, the reason the Presentation Revolution is alive and well is that speakers have not been holding up their end of the bargain. Audiences do their part by giving us the benefit of the doubt; we prove to be idiots, or—dodging that pitfall—arrogant and insensitive jerks. Dodging *that* pitfall, we appear sterile and boring. Dodging

TRUST

IS AN

emotional commitment,

NOT

A

rational decision.

that pitfall . . . you get the point. There's always something, it seems. So how do we get a handle on audience perception?

Credibility is not expertise. Expertise fuels credibility, but they are not synonymous terms. In the presentation world, credibility equates to trust. At times, we trust because of expertise, but there are other elements involved: sincerity, likability, warmth, compatibility, etc. As you know, it's far easier to maintain trust than to build it from scratch, and far easier to build it from scratch than to rebuild it once it is broken. Recognizing the grace that the audience gives you is critical to mastering audience expectations and delivering on credibility.

HOW TO BUILD AND MAINTAIN CREDIBILITY

Like many of you, I drive on roads. Interstates are best, in my view: Give me a wide expanse of asphalt with no traffic lights or pedestrians and let me cover the ground as quickly as possible. No stopping, no looking around. Just pure, single-minded transport. The simplicity is fantastic.

It appears that I'm not the only one who thinks this way. Every day, there are tens of thousands of motorists streaming through the same channels that I am, often at speeds surpassing 70 mph. Though car accidents at 30 mph can be fatal, many of us hop on the interstate with one intention: to get somewhere faster than we could by any other means.

Yet many of us are surviving the drive day after day. In fact, survival rates are so high that we act as if the ritual isn't even dangerous. We send e-mails, we jam to our music, we exact discipline on fighting children, and we eat full meals all while hurtling down the freeway at speeds that surpass our reflexive abilities. We all stay between the lines, so we feel safe. It's amazing what those little, white painted dashes can do. Inches are all that separate us from each other on the interstate, and yet we all dive in every day.

Why do we trust this spidery network of pavement? It's simple: because we're all there together. There is a diffusion of responsibility. We figure that if this many people are traveling at such and such a speed, it *must* be safe. Certain situations put us in herd mode, and the interstate is one of them. It isn't foolishness by any means—because most of the time, the herd is right. Statistically, I know I've been driving among druggies, alcoholics, aggressive maniacs, lawyers, politicians, and so on, yet I have never been harmed. The painted lines create trust: the system is working in my favor and helping me to arrive on time or, at least, less late.

But what do we do when we see a wreck during our normal commute? Do we keep our heads forward, our foot on the gas? As I've complained so often before, we do not. We slow down. We gawk. We (gasp) rubberneck. And the world slows to a halt.

For years, I considered this phenomenon to be proof positive of the sick and depraved human mind. The inconsideration! Don't those rubberneckers know that I have somewhere to be? I could understand a 25 percent reduction in speed to compensate for the loss of one lane on a four-lane interstate, but 70 to 25? It doesn't compute. The gawkers—and I'm as guilty as anyone—have no intention of helping, and the victims probably don't feel like being stared at. On the whole, it equates to a moral catastrophe, one that we witness nearly every day.

Or so I thought.

However, I've come to think that something else is at work. Every day, our trust in the painted lines allows us to perform a remarkable task: propel our vulnerable, soft-skinned bodies at breakneck speeds within inches of semi-trucks and knee-steering, cell phone–jabbering teenagers. Put like that, you'd think only rodeo clowns and backwoods lunatics would voluntarily jump on the road. But it isn't so: Even the intensely phobic come to play. Routine almost always usurps fear.

When we see a wreck, though, that trust is broken. The veneer of the protective painted lines is compromised. We realize that, at 70 mph, serious damage can occur. We do what we would always do were it not for the sort of mass buy-in that convinces us otherwise: we slow down to a manageable speed. We heighten our awareness. We use our blinkers. We watch the road.

For as long as we're witnessing the breach of trust that accidents represent, we maintain this snail's pace. As soon as we pass it, our speed begins to rise. By the time we can't see the wreckage in the mirrors anymore, we're back at 70 mph. The illusion has rebooted.

Your presentation resembles a mass commute: You're trying to get a large group of individuals to go in the same direction at the same speed. Momentum is key, especially as audiences get larger. Small shifts in momentum—a sudden tap on the brakes, a technical difficulty—can hugely affect the time it takes to move your audience from point A to point B. So long as you are painting the lines and keeping the vehicles inside them, the perception of credibility is present. It's smooth sailing. Take your eyes off the road or drop your awareness for a moment, and you may find your presentation stuck in bumper-to-bumper traffic for as far as the eye can see.

You're building and maintaining trust, appealing to emotions to set the stage for cold, hard facts. We build on the fundamental trust we receive when we walk into the room, and we maintain the momentum that trust provides. We're hardwired to trust certain qualities and distrust others. It's your job to represent those honorable qualities. The more favorably that you, your work, or your company are known, the more likely it is that you'll walk into presentations with a heightened level of implied authority, much more so than an unknown, unproved competitor. While fame and notoriety will give you a leg up, don't count solely on them; continue to exude trustworthy qualities before, during, and after the presentation. If you don't have a large platform, you need to focus especially on building trust during those precious first moments of the presentation. Every presentation situation requires that you employ three can't-skip practices in order to build and maintain trust. You absolutely must convey the following qualities to the audience.

Be Genuine

Unless you are a famous soap opera star who reached the top by pretending to be a steamy doctor, you are on stage because of the expertise you possess—and, to put it more roundly, who you are. *You* are the one who is speaking instead of 5, 10, or 100 other potential candidates because of everything you represent: your story, achievements, determination, and goals. It's okay for the audience to want more than the raw information because the story is really about your relationship to the data. It's how we understand what numbers and trends mean. It's also how we trust. Otherwise, every self-proclaimed, "attractive, successful single person seeking lifelong partner" on eHarmony would have already been snatched up. They're still out there though, which suggests that there is more than plain information to every story. Let your personal quirks and history shine through. They make you human, and audiences trust humans.

Be Factual

I know, I know; we began the chapter acknowledging that empirical data doesn't equate to credibility, and now I've made it a requirement of building and maintaining trust with your audience. But beware of a mindset that treats data as the all-important reason for your presentation. If your audience had wanted "just the facts," they would have had you e-mail your slide deck to them. They've asked you to appear in person because they need to see you interact with your data. Thus, empirical data is incomplete without your life-giving presence: You give the statistics, charts, and graphs meaning. It isn't just *explaining* what they mean; it's conveying how they should make the audience feel. Being factual is one part honest data and one part honest you. Put them together and the audience will feel as though the numbers really add up.

Be Giving

Audiences can spot an agenda a mile away. Who among us doesn't have premonitions the moment before we are invited into a casual acquaintance's pyramid scheme? There's something in the voice, the body language, or the verbiage that tips us off right away. We run like mad for the exits when we spot this sort of behavior.

Life is about contribution; as The Beatles put it, "In the end, the love you take is equal to the love you make." We need to purify our motives before we step behind the dais. Beyond snaring a big commission check, what can you do for your audience? Are there skills you can impart? Meaningful life lessons? Levity and a break from a stressful day? Your job isn't to save the world, but you can start approaching your presentations with a giving perspective. It's okay to make millions of dollars as you do it. Just make sure you give something back.

We need trust to survive. As I mentioned previously, none of us have the time to pore through an expert's record every time we need advice. At some point, we have to summarize the proof and make a judgment call. Building and maintaining credibility and trust helps your audience make that call early and in your favor. Making your approach more human, taking the time to research your content, and finding a way to provide something meaningful to every audience you address are great tactics for inspiring trust. You set the stage for a successful presentation, but more importantly, you set the stage for a successful relationship.

THEY'RE JUST NOT THAT INTO YOU

The way the audience reacted to your emotional story about how instrumental your mother was in helping you navigate the teenage years was something special. When you told them you still talk to her three times a day, a few began to cry. It gave you goose bumps. What a connection!

And then there were the hilarious moments. You laughed so hard telling the story about your cat dying. Sure, Mr. Pickles was a friend, but being run over by a steamroller? You just can't make that stuff up. It's always nice to entertain an audience.

What a relief: The big presentation is over. The account? Come to think of it, you haven't heard from anyone for days. They never faxed the contract. You make a follow-up call and . . . what? They've decided to go with the competition? What went wrong?

They're just not that into you. I see it all the time: Presenters get so wrapped up in their own experience of the presentation that they forget to put themselves in the audience's shoes. The diatribe about your mother came across to a roomful of people who don't know you as very, very weird. The cat story? Horrific. Most of the people in the room were silent, but you couldn't hear the crickets over your own raucous laughter.

Passion and enthusiasm are absolute must-haves in a presentation. Without them, the audience feels as though they're being lightly slapped with a cold, dead trout for an hour. However, engaging with our material in this way is new, completely uncharted

O2-E

Be watchful of **O-2E** since he is
"offensive to everyone."

territory for some of us. Without a script to follow, we can get lost very quickly. So how do we keep ourselves grounded?

It begins with making a habit of presenting. Well-planned content isn't great content until it is executed well. Constant feedback and adjustments help make the most of great prose and logic. Without serial presenting, you're liable to fall into the same old traps: working hard, thinking you've got a good read on the audience, and losing to the competition. Establishing a *true* connection with the audience is an art, a sixth sense that requires you to be both energetic and interactive with your content while keeping one ear and one eye attuned to the audience at all times. Without both, you may find that you've done an excellent job of entertaining yourself and a horrible job of moving the audience from one place to another.

CRACK THE WINDOWS AND LEAVE YOUR EGO IN THE CAR

Egos are man's best friend. They pick us up when we're feeling down. They love us unconditionally. They give us a sense of purpose and destiny. Companionship like this can only happen when the mind loves itself. And size matters when it comes to egos: the bigger, the better. Right?

Yes—as long as you leave your ego at home. Much like dogs, man's other best friend, egos aren't welcome everywhere. They're relegated to our homes, personal space, and the occasional trip to the park. Elsewhere they need to be on a leash, or otherwise absent. Simply put, other people don't want to sit around stroking your ego. They may not even be ego people; they may be humility people, who probably have cats.

Whether or not you think cat people are weird, the reality is that they exist and we have to live our lives around them. The same goes for humility people: If you must bring your ego with you as you travel the speaking circuit, it is imperative that you leave it in the car. Crack the windows, leave a bowl of water and a squeaky toy, and go do your presentation. Bringing the ego up on stage is as appropriate as bringing a dog with you. Please don't be that guy.

Egos are fundamentally inward-focused. No matter how often you remind yourself to think of others, the ego acts like a colored veil, forcing you to see the world in terms of me, myself, and mine. If you want to deliver great content, you have to prevent the audience from suspecting that your ego is involved.

However, if we get too hung up on everything we're *not* supposed to do, the creative process suffers. Too many restrictions can cause the more imaginative side of our brains to seize up and suck its thumb for hours. How do we safeguard our processes to prevent the ego from slipping into our content?

Instead of falling into this trap, simply set aside a stage in the revision process where every element of the content is examined for ego. There is a fine line here: Building credibility can quickly turn into bragging, but your audience needs to know your capabilities and qualifications. Use your best judgment, and make a habit of polling the audience (or otherwise soliciting anonymous feedback) so that you can begin to heighten your sixth sense of audience connections.

Remember: you serve your content, and your content serves your objective. If you've done a good job clarifying the objectives, you should always have a suitable litmus test available. As you're examining your statements and claims or deciding what information to include and what to cut, consider what the content points to. Every bit of information is present to accomplish the objective. Keep this in the forefront of your mind and you can bask in the glory of your successful presentations after the Q&A.

GENUINE AUTHENTICITY

Our 44th president, Barack Obama, is a master of authenticity. Though the country seems to be divided on the politics of his administration, few people question his powerful presence on stage and among the people. An unlikely candidate at the outset of the 2008 Presidential Campaign, his ability to connect with ordinary citizens quickly propelled him to the front of the pack. How does he do it?

Perhaps more than any other politician, Obama looks at home with his constituents, often answering unexpected questions off the cuff with thoughtful, non-rote answers. A genial smile, an empathetic frown, and an ear turned forward to listen are oftentimes all it takes to communicate sincerity and genuine concern to another human being. These simple, everyday qualities have been instrumental in taking a poor Hawaiian boy all the way to the White House.

START MAKING A

HABIT

OF

imagining life

FROM

another person's

*point
of view.*

Undoubtedly, there will be some who are hesitant to take inspiration from the man. The nature of modern politics makes it so. But remember Bruce Lee's example: If a Kung Fu master is willing to learn from professional wrestlers, surely we can learn from the Republicans and Democrats who communicate genuine authenticity better than the rest.

How can you connect so authentically? Are you as comfortable out among the audience as you are on stage? Do you work hard to establish a meeting of the minds? Empathy is a powerful presentation tool, but so often our pride gets in the way. We don't practice taking others' perspectives and, in the end, we suffer for it.

Start making a habit of imagining life from another person's point of view. Your presentations will take on a new level of emotional interaction that is vital to establishing credibility and rapport.

DON THE WHITE COAT

Don't let that expensive Italian suit fool you: You are the servant, and the audience is the master. They invited you. They signed the check. They cleared their schedules and suspended countless potential work hours to hear you say what you have to say. To be fair, you've been working hard yourself: clarifying, brainstorming, outlining, revising, and practicing, practicing, practicing. Really, the lengths we'll go to in order to hear someone speak, or to speak to someone, are pretty amazing.

There's no faster way to turn bated breath to halitosis than to show up looking for spa treatment. At the worst presentation

I ever attended, the keynote speaker spent 20 minutes of a 30-minute slot explaining, in great detail, his academic pedigree and personal achievements. The moral of the story was that more individuals in society should aspire to be like him, or even just a tenth of the man he fancied himself to be. Needless to say, we all walked away quite determined to forget everything he had said.

When we step on stage, we need to imagine that we're putting on a white service coat. How can we help the audience? How can we meet their top needs and desires expeditiously? This approach covers so many presentation sins, even (dare I say) the sin of using bullet-pointed lists. The people roaming about the world today are hungry for connections. We have a million technological devices that provide a semblance of relationships, but very few of us ever feel truly loved, listened to, or respected. When you, the speaker, show up on stage and display a genuine interest in your audience's well-being and advancement, you create energy in the room that is fueled and sustained by the very welcome feeling of real, meaningful interaction with another human being.

The trick, of course, is not learning how to do it. That part is easy: you just put others first. The trick is remembering to *try*. This sort of interaction is a dying art in our society, which is simultaneously saddening and thrilling. It's saddening in that we see evidence of relational hunger every day in the news; loneliness, frustration, and depression are an increasingly prevalent part of many people's daily cycles of emotions. It's thrilling because this void creates a huge opportunity for motivated, big-picture people to step in and start meeting needs.

Start each day—and certainly each presentation—seeking to reach common ground with your audience. The momentum you gain from this effort will more than justify the investment of time it takes; no matter what happens with your discussion, you'll impress a very positive mark on their minds as you leave. Although it may be hard to see the short-term payoff, these unquantifiable opportunities carry an enormous amount of potential for your message. Your efforts will not go unrewarded.

Chapter 7

They Matter Even More

I'll allow for the fact that not everyone reading this book is a die-hard perfectionist. But I think I can safely assume that, given the choice between a perfect presentation and abject failure, we'd all choose the former. Only a premier slacker would purposefully sabotage a presentation, and even then it would beg the question: Why bother? If you hate your job that much, why even show up to take the dive?

With this widely accommodating standard of universal ambition in mind, it's high time we take a look at this slippery term, "perfect." Personal tastes color ideals across the board; food, art, humor, politics, family values, and more are all subject to individuals' whims and life experiences. Yet we are engaging in mass communication when we present—albeit a slightly targeted version. Someone in the room will like modern design; someone will think it's too edgy. Someone would have preferred vegetarian options for lunch; someone is searching for the burgers. With so many variables at work, it's a wonder that anyone reaches a level of appeal beyond the immediate family, and even then . . . well, that's a different book entirely.

This is the reason I'm excited about the iPad: One day, perhaps everyone will tote one of these personal entertainment devices around, allowing us to deliver messages based on user-specific information with pinpoint accuracy. However, until then, we have to carry on with lots and lots of assumptions, some of which will be very, very broad and unspecific. We're going to treat audiences of 25, 50, even 1,000 people as if they were one organism. It isn't fair, and it doesn't do them justice. But at the end of the day, our job is to move the entire herd from one place to another. And there's simply no viable way of doing this individually.

Ah, the faceless masses: No matter how much time you spend brainstorming, no matter how sweet and natural your non-verbal gestures are, and no matter how mesmerizing your lofty prose may be, you are going to miss hard if you can't put a face on those masses. In fact, it will physically hurt how much you will miss. Trust me; I've been there.

So how do we create content that feels personal even as it sears the fingerprints off of their hands?

We begin by making a choice between two options. Life is either meaningless, individuality is sacred, and we trade our laser pointers for Wii controllers to ride out our futile existences in the pursuit of staggering hand-screen coordination or we commit to just do the best we can to make our content meaningful to as many individuals in the audience as possible. Feel free to set this book down to think about it for a while. Maybe even take the day off.

When your fingernails turn white as you clinch the laser pointer in a moment of determined commitment and stand to pursue uncompromising greatness, I have some good news: We have plenty of sociological data available that can help target our message. Everyone is an individual, but groups of individuals— called generations—undergo the same historical moments together. Their shared experiences have a way of consolidating individuality, so that despite the vintage, one-of-a-kind clothing we all seek out, we still end up being very similar to one another. We are complicit in uniformity by our desire for individuality, if nothing else. And that's where the presenter's first sure footing lays.

Knowing your audience is more of a dark art than a science—a composite of generational assumptions, tenuous occupational generalizations, and mystical leaf-readings that make witches' brews look like the medium-roast option at your local Starbucks. You'll almost certainly find yourself globetrotting throughout the world, searching for amulets and ancient texts that allow you to divine the single approach Mother Earth would want you to use when speaking to her children. You'll need a messenger bag, plus the confidence to wear it, even when your friends call it a purse.

Just kidding! Knowing your audience is easy. An awareness of generational tendencies can certainly shorten the learning curve substantially, but we're ultimately talking about good ol' fashioned empathy: walking a mile in another man's shoes, living life on the other side of the tracks, broadening your horizons, and so on. We have to let our common sense and intuition trump unfeeling rules. For example, the Millennial Generation, like every generation before it, carries its share of stigmas and unfair characterizations; research suggests that these up-and-comers are entitled, unaccustomed to hard work, and spoiled.

Demographics, generational studies, & OTHER *social analytics tools* ARE JUST THAT:

TOOLS.

THEY ARE **not** *laws.*

THEY ARE **not** *rules.*

THEY ARE **not** *inscribed on tablets.*

So please don't treat them as if they are.

Regardless, as a presenter you can probably assume that a roomful of debate team captains from around the country will be motivated workaholics, just like all debate team captains since the dawn of time. Demographics, generational studies, and other social analytics tools are just that: tools. They are not laws. They are not rules. They are not inscribed on tablets. So please don't treat them as if they are.

There. You've been warned. So how do we effectively address our presentations to our target audience?

Why don't we look to potatoes for guidance?

In the run-up to the war in Iraq, the American Congress voted to enact legislation changing the unpatriotically named French fries to the more savory Freedom fries. The name fits in establishment Washington, where the predominance of bureaucrats are Baby Boomers who rose from the ashes of WWII, trudged through the muck of the Cold War, and endured the economic turbulence of the late 70s and early 80s. Baby Boomers love freedom and most probably hate France. Thus, Freedom fries was a nicely targeted rebranding.

Meanwhile, in every gentrified neighborhood across America, hipsters—the representative counterculture of the Millennial Generation—are gathering in large numbers. Their pseudo-dive restaurants serve local, organic, tempura-fried heirloom potatoes, indicative of the guiding moral and socioeconomic trends that have shaped these mysterious creatures' preferences in recent years. What would those Boomers in Washington do with such taters? Likely, they would have put a plateful before a congressional hearing and vetted them for public service. And the hipsters, what would they do with Freedom fries? Undoubtedly, they would compost them.

Before we get hung up on whether or not these assumptions are fair, let's focus on the big picture: If you're a regional representative for Ore-Ida looking for some large french fry accounts, there is a wide swath of wiggle room in which you can tailor your presentation to fit the audience. Incorporating some basic common sense regarding your collective audience's probable leanings will give your presentation a truly personal feel.

We do need to be aware of the pitfalls: Target your presentation too much, and you may alienate outliers—people who may well be key decision makers. If you yourself are not representative of the group you're addressing, too much specification can come across as pandering. We're trying to convey a reasonable amount of empathy to the audience, not a complete understanding of everything that motivates them. The former is endearing; the latter is offensive.

Tailoring a presentation to the audience takes sensitivity and practice. I find the easiest method is to start with macro-categories—generations, genders, classes, and sectors—and then start to look at micro-categories—education, artistic preferences, regional considerations, and so on. From macro to micro, I jot down the categories that apply to my audience. For each category, I make notes about emotional hot spots, taboos, tendencies, and competencies. This gives me a clear picture of the tone and angle I want for my presentation, which in turn gives me great confidence on stage.

CONNECTING WITH MILLENNIALS

Everyone is trying to reach these so-called slacker elites, and everyone is consistently failing to do so. The result has been an exasperated profusion of op-ed dismay over a work force that has hardly passed the fetal stage. The Millennial classification includes individuals between the ages of 13 and 30, approximately. That means that although this generation has, at best, less than 10 years of active work experience, we have already branded them unfit for duty.

Meanwhile, the businesses, movements, and politicians that are embracing these youngsters are thriving. Millennials tend to be extremely loyal to brands, motivated by morals and ethics over dollars and cents (think Whole Foods versus Walmart), and technologically savvy. Facebook, Twitter, and blogosphere campaigns disseminate staggeringly in-depth ideals and information to large cohorts of this generation in minutes or even seconds. If you push a Millennial's button, they'll post it, tweet it, and blog about it. That goes for the good and the bad.

Push a Boomer's button, by comparison, and they'll tell a neighbor—maybe two. Sure, there are some technologically savvy members of this generation as well, but the compounded power of word of mouth is decidedly concentrated among Millennials. Therefore, your goal is to get this group actively involved on your behalf. It's foolish to write them off as over-privileged since these people will work for you free of charge in the realm of social media. It's sort of ridiculous, like hiring squirrels to crack nuts for you and *having them like it*.

Consider the changes in technology that have occurred over the past 13–30 years: Where was the Internet three decades ago? What could it do? How difficult/expensive was an international phone call? If you wanted to find a recipe for piecrust, where did you go? If you needed to write a report on tigers, where could you look? If you missed your favorite show one night, what were your options?

The forbearers of the Millennial generation precipitated all of these changes; now that they embody the full measure of these advancements, many individuals resent them. We have to understand that Millennials don't view absolute technological saturation as anything other than a fact of life, like grass or air. They are accustomed to having everything they need right at their fingertips. They learned to read with wireless connectivity-enabled Leap Frog pens that scanned and read the words they didn't understand. They're accordingly confident in their ability to figure things out. Sometimes this can come across as entitlement; other times, they seem more resourceful than any other generation. A new Millennial in the office is far more likely to answer his own questions online than an older worker. They detest the obvious and the redundant. They expect to use the full range of technological capabilities in everything they do: work, play, and apparently even sleep (judging from the iPhone's sleep noise app).

Members of this generation have witnessed a shocking amount of corporate irresponsibility, from Enron to the recent financial meltdown, and a good deal of social change, too. Movies like *Food, Inc.* and *Fast Food Nation* have been extremely successful among Millennials, who have no problem paying $5/lb for ground beef when $2/lb is available. They're not necessarily wealthy or financially privileged, but they do have a tendency to value ideals and principles over raw (no pun intended) financial concerns.

Reaching Millennials isn't rocket science; however, it does require some pronounced perspective taking if you are in your mid-30s or older. For brevity's sake, we'll assume that the 12 and under crowd isn't presenting just yet. The following are some of the common roadblocks to reaching this new generation.

The Prince

In his renowned work, Machiavelli stated that a prince would display more grace in losing a father than an inheritance. Managers all across the country are wrestling with a similar perception of the Millennials in the workforce today. The complaint I hear most often is that these young professionals don't work as hard, arrive with a sense of entitlement every day, and don't respect authority.

In reality, the situation is far more nuanced. Statistically speaking, Millennials were raised in two-income families and grew up doing more things for themselves. They may not know much about business, but their bent is self-sufficiency. They'll Google what they don't know; asking the Boss is a last resort. Though it may sound counterintuitive, activating Millennials requires placing far *more* responsibilities on their shoulders. Overwhelm them with directives, not rules. Give them clear and incredibly lofty objectives, and encourage them to simply get the job done. They'll want to work from home (using the technology they're so familiar with), so try it out: clearly establish what needs to be done, and hold them accountable to their results. You may be surprised at how much they're willing to work given this sort of freedom.

Use some of these same guidelines in the presentation setting. If you have activities or discussions you want to foster, don't waste their time in a stuffy auditorium. Instead, try sending them home to continue the discussion online. Generate passion and enthusiasm for the ideals you're discussing; don't overload them with easy-access information. If you sell them a value, they'll join the relevant Facebook group and stay up till 1 a.m. reading about it online.

Most importantly, make certain that any presentation you deliver to a group of Millennials has an extremely clear objective: lay the standard and hold them accountable to the necessary action. If you're selling a product or service, focus on the underlying values that differentiate your product from a competitor's—especially if that competitor is a larger corporation. And if you're the corporation, be sure to play up stories pertaining to your company's beginnings, when it was just another Mom & Pop store somewhere in Middle America. Remember, their world is connected and everything is local. You should be, too.

No Waiting

Millennials spent half of their educational careers watching adults fumble through Windows operating systems, trying to demonstrate exciting new technology. From a young age, they were more proficient than their instructors, in much the same way that a two-year-old learning English and Spanish has an easier time than the high school or college student taking Spanish 101. Their brains are wired for immediate access in a way that many of us cannot even fathom. The good news is that we don't have to catch up; we just have to incorporate these notions into that with our presentations.

Millennials are not likely to value the buildup; they've seen every movie, heard every song, read every story, and so on. They have been suffused with culture for the duration of their lives, so don't walk into the presentation expecting to blow their minds. Instead, challenge them on values. Millennials seek values systems that are consistent across all of the areas of their lives: social, occupational, spiritual, and educational.

In my personal experience, I have found that Millennials are far more receptive to overt challenges than other generations, but far less tolerant of an elaborate story.

The lesson, then, is to approach the presentation with intensity and focus. Put them in the back seat, buckle them in, and get the car going 50 mph or faster—high-speed enough to discourage bailing. Keep the foot on the gas, too. You may finish your presentation early, but who cares? They're trying to figure out why you're not web conferencing with them from home in the first place.

MILLENNIALS

SEEK *value systems* THAT ARE

constant

ACROSS **ALL** OF THE
AREAS OF THEIR LIVES:

*social,
occupational,
spiritual, &
educational.*

Great Expectations

With an idealist generation comes a lofty checklist for presenters. Millennials trend metaphysical: They experience the greatest amount of friction with their managers over issues of purpose, destiny, and dreams. They're not going to understand why they shouldn't have the opportunity to be deeply and morally engaged with what they do at a very early point in their careers. Remember, for them, the world has been "flat" for decades. Moving across the Atlantic for a job is not too different from moving across the state, and they're inclined to seek one-of-a-kind experiences over the ordinary or the secure.

We can either beat our heads against the wall in frustration as we bicker over whether or not a 26-year-old has the right to enjoy working from home instead of from an office, or we can accept that this is a changing reality in today's work culture and take advantage of it. What better a time to raise the bar for productivity and quality than at the exact moment that you bestow upon your Millennials their coveted autonomy? You can test me on this: The next time you have to communicate with a group of Millennials, try bartering freedom for great expectations. The one thing you do *not* want to do is approach them in an authoritarian manner, focusing on minutia and ignoring the big picture. It may be how you were raised to think, but it's far easier to change our own approach than it is to change a generation. We have to gain influence before we can impart values.

Plugging In

If you're not too technologically savvy yourself, you should seriously consider involving a Millennial during your brainstorming session. Specifically, engage him or her in discovering new ways of making your presentation content interactive. What are the possibilities on Facebook? Twitter? Blogs? Can you demonstrate certain claims by having a member of the audience use their iPhone to prove information on the spot? Because an audience composed of teens to 20-somethings is going to start twitching for their Woobies about 10 minutes after you take the stage, I advise all to put offense aside and get them tapping with you instead of at you. Imagine the sort of reach and publicity you can get just by asking them to share your key message through their preferred social media outlet. They'll be so relieved to have their electronics back out where they can see them that they'll likely generate thousands of free impressions of your company to everyone they know.

The faster we start thinking about Millennials' strengths rather than their weaknesses, the faster we can tap into the power of this up-and-coming generation for the benefit of our messages.

CONNECTING WITH GENERATION X

If they don't have gray hair but still wear collared shirts, chances are they're members of Generation X. Our age doesn't smell like teen spirit anymore; it smells like mortgages, bald spots, and varicose veins—and we don't like it. Our grunge bands were the hardest rockers since the 70s, and it's hard to see that chip on the shoulder be buffed out by the sands of time.

However, we're starting to run the show. We're in our mid-30s on up, and every time a Baby Boomer retires, one of us gets a corner office. Though we're tech savvy, technology doesn't suffuse every part of our lives. In fact, many of us are trying to find a boundary between work and play; unlike Millennials, we expect a divide.

For the first time in American history we earn, on average, less money than our parents did, which we did before making less money than your parents was cool. There is some definite overlap between Xs and Millennials: The rise of technology more or less defines us; we are confident and idealistic; we're snooty about coffee. But Xs are in a markedly different place in life right now. We now have families, established careers, and retirement goals.

You'll notice that none of the above qualities are very "grungy." Generation X isn't joined at the hip with values and ideals. There's wiggle room here, and despite witnessing the flattening of the world, we still envision ourselves as individuals, whereas Millennials tend to feel like they are parts of various movements. We're far more likely to be motivated by our own world—our job, family, home—than we are the world "out there." This small difference can have an extraordinary impact on the way we perceive presentations. Here are some approaches for connecting with Generation X.

Tell, Don't Sell

Though Xs are certainly *capable* of finding all the relevant information on a given topic, it's not really what we prefer to do. Despite a familiarity with Google, we'd still like to learn from an expert; call us old-fashioned.

DESPITE A
familiarity
WITH **Google,**

WE'D STILL LIKE TO
LEARN FROM AN

EXPERT;
*call us old
fashioned.*

At the same time, we possess the same sort of confidence as our younger compatriots in our ability to learn and interpret data. That confidence engenders a certain resistance to being spoon-fed. If Millennials were raised in two-income households, we are the generation everyone experimented with to see if that would work. We can do things on our own; we just appreciate the help.

In a sense, the presentation strategy for Xs is reversed compared with Millennials: instead of providing an aerial view of ideals augmented with a clear and decisive objective, provide the information that illustrates your point and allow us to come to our own conclusion. Sure, it's just for show: We know you've loaded the deck so that the only logical decision is your product or service. We just don't want you to say it out loud.

The Need for Speed

If the content is right, Xs have the capacity and processing power to move through it quickly. We were raised on MTV and Oliver Stone: you wouldn't think that would predispose a group of individuals to rapid-fire statistics and empirical data, but it does. We understand the issues. We understand our values. What we want from you is a collage of supporting evidence for what you say we should be doing.

Call it arrogance or haste, but in the end it simply *is*: Reaching Xs is about equipping us with the raw materials. Like Millennials, we expect to do most things ourselves. Unlike Millennials, we were raised by parents who trusted in the nightly news. We're still comfortable getting facts from an authoritative source, but we rarely trust that source enough to take our opinions from it as well.

Presenting to Xs is a true service, not a performance: organize your thesis carefully and keep the data extremely relevant. We'll take the entertainment—we're still the fun-loving teenagers of the early 90s in our hearts—but it should never be a leading player in the presentation flow. Keep it light and passing, spending the majority of the time really digging down deep into the evidence; we'll track you every step of the way.

Rage against the Machine

Sure, we all grew up: We cut our grunge hair, ditched the Doc Martens for dress shoes, and put down our Stratocasters to take up leather briefcases. While you can take the X out of the grunge scene, you can't take the grunge out of the X. The social revolution we all stood behind may have cracked and faded, but our tenure as iconoclasts has left an indelible mark on our hearts. Though we're out in the real world now, those streaks of idealism remain. We're still inclined to mistrust corporations and bureaucracy, and we're responsible for informing the small-scale, local sensibilities that the Millennials now embrace.

That doesn't mean a corporation can't reach Generation X. Indeed, one of the best examples of a company mastering Gen X messaging is Starbucks, a huge corporation that nevertheless continues to enjoy X support in large numbers. We know Starbucks is "the Man," but it's engaged in and promoted a social agenda that we love. From a purely business perspective, one could argue that there are few differences between Starbucks and McDonald's: Both are expanding rapidly, capitalizing on uniformity and ubiquity, and making life difficult for small mom-and-pops stores everywhere. Xs have withdrawn from

McDonald's but embraced Starbucks, for one simple reason: Starbucks appears charitable and socially responsible, but McDonald's does not. My generation's dollars can flow anywhere: when presenting to a roomful of Xs, make every effort to deliver pragmatic facts with a social (rather than corporate) vision and you'll be able to lead us wherever you want us to go.

Boom Times

The country's most populous generation ever, Baby Boomers are responsible for nearly every artifact of modern culture for a very simple reason: they have occupied nearly every public office, management position, and teacher's desk for decade after decade. They came of age sandwiched between two defining wars, WWII and Vietnam, and developed an ideology that shaped both themselves and the nation. They saw the ending of FDR's era; capitulated back to a free market, corporate-centered system; and at their height were the driving force behind the money-glamorizing 1980s.

Anchor the Stage

The average Baby Boomer still expects a news anchor to be a journalist. Boomers are not quite sure about the talking head cable news shift that has taken place of late. This is telling: They're looking for substance that's wrapped up in a highly credible source. The more Boomers in your audience, the more you'll be expected to tout personal achievements, qualifications, and a tremendous amount of credibility. In other words, Boomers consider the source to be equal to the information. If you're trustworthy and reliable, what you say will be trustworthy and reliable.

I love presenting to Baby Boomers because of a very simple fact that I believe stems from the way they grew up getting news: Boomers have incredible attention spans. At times, presenting to the technology-saturated younger generations can feel a bit like a slash-and-dash job, as if I'm cutting up information into bite-sized bits of entertainment rather than engaging in true discourse on a given topic. To be fair, I love the challenge of meeting today's generation of innovative idealists, but finding myself in a roomful of Boomers with an hour to spend swimming in the deep end of any topic is intensely refreshing. Perhaps my generation and the one before us will grow into an appreciation of depth over style; but in case we don't, I would advise you to take full advantage of the unique attention a Baby Boomer audience can give you. Stretch yourself: Try to make your content deeper, even more analytical and honest than it usually is. A Boomer talk is vastly stimulating and will do wonders for advancing your ability to peel back the layers of your typical discussions.

College Bound

Thanks to the Boomers, scores of Millennials now grab undergraduate degrees with as much thought as moving from eighth to ninth grade. Baby Boomers were the first generation to seek advancement through education in large figures. More importantly, they were the generation that saw advanced education begin to become accessible to the middle and even lower classes.

Even more importantly, Boomers have incorporated their educations into their careers. Younger generations have had more trouble translating college experience into the workforce, in part due to the effects of globalization and the outsourcing that has made certain collegiate skills replicable and cheap. Your Boomer audience is far more likely to expect an appeal to their training during a presentation, whereas a younger generation will perceive a presentation as an opportunity to learn something brand new. Boomers are at an age of self-actualization and wisdom accumulation; younger generations are still seeking skills and knowledge that will solidify careers and lifestyles. Thus, when speaking to a predominantly older demographic, it would be wise to speak to them as if they already possess a great deal of the requisite training and knowledge—and make it clear that you're merely there to enhance and add to their familiarity with the subject matter.

When Apple Was Macintosh

Boomers have seen technological advancements that were every bit as revolutionary as iPads, Skype, and so on. But they witnessed these advancements as fully formed adults in most cases, and the advancements tended to be more infrastructural and less application-based in their implementation. Boomers worked for corporations that had fully-staffed technology departments that handled all technological matters. Today, securing an entry-level position almost anywhere requires a thorough understanding of modern technology, and IT deals with web sites and interactivity instead of raw processing power.

While it is entirely possible for a Boomer to be extremely proficient with modern technology, as a generation, they're not likely to demand it. A single expert speaking at length on a relevant subject will do just fine; don't spend hours trying to incorporate interactivity and Twitter feeds into your presentation outline. Spend that time building a thoroughly researched, heavily themed argument.

Like Wine and Cheese

Pay attention to the next commercial you see targeted at the 50+ demographic. Aging isn't fading; aging is reinventing. Thanks to advances in modern medicine, Boomers can expect to live several decades beyond retirement. They may be retiring, but they're often doing so to pursue second, legacy-building professional lives. Increasingly more Boomers retire to assume educational, charitable, or religious posts. At the same time, they're likely to take up new or long-forgotten hobbies—sailing, tennis, fly-fishing, and so forth.

Boomers have extremely high expectations for post-retirement. Treating them as if they'll exit the working world at 65 could quite possibly be the worst mistake you could make during a presentation.

Focus instead on legacy and how the skills and information you're delivering has implications far outside of their professional lives. They're big-picture people these days; your content should be, too.

Don't Let World Views Collide

Boomers spent some time in youthful resistance, and they certainly didn't perpetuate the extreme social conservatism of their parents (a breed unto themselves, but, being in retirement,

TREATING THEM AS IF THEY'LL

exit the working world at

65

COULD QUITE POSSIBLY BE THE

worst mistake

you could make during a presentation.

rarely presented to anymore). They didn't cling to their youth the way the generations that followed them have, however. Boomers are as likely to view an appeal to social justice as dubious or misleading when selling a product or service; as far as they are concerned, the two don't mix. Boomers are far more comfortable with compartments, whereas Xs and Millennials increasingly seek an integrated existence across all facets of human life.

Speaking to this older audience can be much less nuanced, and much more to the point, then. Don't worry about pitching your product as anything other than a high-quality product that does exactly what it's supposed to do. Lawn mowers mow lawns; they don't save starving children while doing so. They'll understand that the world is changing, but world-is-flat thinking isn't the reality that governed most of their lives. That's today's reality, and today's Boomers are handing off their responsibilities to the younger generations in greater numbers every day.

The Over-Simplification Trap

Even if you did manage to get an audience that so neatly fit into one of the three generations discussed earlier, you can still get into trouble by assuming uniformity. Despite the times that raised us, we all want to be treated like significant individuals, not cows in a herd. Every chair in the room is filled with a person who will absorb your content and make a decision in response: to either to go along with you or not. Few approaches are more repulsive than cookie-cutter presentations; you need to create an environment that is appealing and accessible to everybody.

COOKIE CUTTER

Being status quo won't "cut" it.

Baby Boomers won't be offended if you incorporate mobile interactivity into your presentation; Millennials won't jitter and explode if you pedal on a subject for more than two minutes. Audiences have a way of stepping up to a presenter's expectations. If you approach the presentation scenario with confidence, they're likely to go along.

At the same time, incorporating some of these high-altitude generalizations can help you create that sense of belonging and mutual empathy to move large groups of people to action. Use tact when doing so: A magician never reveals his secrets because it ruins the show, and such is the presenter's task. We have to put our best foot forward and try to make every audience member feel equally loved and appreciated. We can't reveal to them all of the assumptions that lead to our approach. Never presume to "understand" someone, but always seek to. Audiences love the effort but hate the assumption.

You're also going to face a million other variables: extroversion versus introversion; ponderous versus impulsive; had a good morning versus had a bad morning; even tall versus short. The goal of this chapter is not to drive you into hiding behind the projection screen until everyone leaves somewhat awkwardly; it is to get you thinking about your content in terms of audience makeup. If we don't consider the audience, we'll simply organize and deliver our content according to our own likes, dislikes, and preferences. Hopefully, we would already do business with ourselves given the opportunity and wouldn't need such formal convincing.

Start thinking about your audience: Who are they? What motivates them? What is their collective experience with your message, if they have any at all? Practice understanding your audience on a very deep level, and I promise it will take practice. You'll find, over time, that your content takes on a laser-like focus that is far more effective in reaching audiences than anything you've tried up to this point.

Chapter 8

Styles and Approaches

Have you ever noticed that there is no such thing as an uncreative child? Take a look around the next time you're at the park: How many briefcases do you see? Are any three-year-olds taking meeting notes so that there is a record of the day's play? Are any of the children in the sandbox pontificating about style guide violations?

Of course, by the time children reach grade school, we adults have usually found a way to tamp down their wild spirit. Cars don't have mouths. Grass can't be pink. Alligators don't have sheep heads. Blah, blah, blah.

I've never been able to discover what adults love so much about conformity. Maybe it's the month-by-month pressure of bills that leads us to crave predictability. Or maybe we trade the pursuit of novel excitement for stability (try as we might). Whatever it is that leads us to shun creativity, it is a thorough impulse that happens to nearly all of us. Reclaiming the free-spirited brain of youth takes a concerted level of energy and practice; however, it is a vital step in the quest for presentation god status.

The first thing we need to do is rethink our definition of creativity. If it means the ability to create something new or unseen, then why have we been designating landscape artists as creative? If it means, quite simply, having the ability to create a tangible object of any sort—be it art, furniture, writing, songs—then why do we consider a philosopher's ideas so creative? The truth is, most of our assumptions about what is and is not creative are handed down, generation after generation, without a second thought as to accuracy, consistency, or relevance. If we feel we fit the archetypal creative mold, we live with the sense that we are, indeed, creative. If we somehow do not, we surrender the benefits of creative living to others.

I see this trend frequently among businesspeople. Business is hardly considered an art, yet millions upon millions of businesspeople create marketing programs, new products or services, more efficient organizational structures—the list goes on and on—every single day. Years ago, upon recognizing that nearly everyone with whom I came in contact was creative in some respect, I began to develop a new, more inclusive definition of creativity, one that didn't reserve the honorable distinction for prodigious and eccentric hermits living in the backwoods of the Rocky Mountains, for instance.

My definition is this: Creativity is problem solving. It fits across the board: The landscape painter identifies a problem—that a beautiful scene is fleeting and changeable—and seeks to capture it on canvas. The philosopher is keenly aware of a logical inconsistency and seeks to address it in the mind. The businessman recognizes an unmet desire in society and brings a remedy to market. If we are going to transmit our ideas to one another, we first need to cultivate a sincere confidence that our ideas are worth their weight in gold. Imagine if Michelangelo had lacked the confidence to put his heart and soul into the Sistine Chapel account or if Andy Warhol had deferred to the style of other, more "creative" people. The first quality of humanity's greatest creative minds is not creativity; that elusive first quality is confidence.

Begin to separate creativity and execution in your mind. Creativity is about solving a problem; for example, you need the board's support for a new human resources campaign. How can you get board members to follow you? Execution is the sterile, technical implementation of your creative ideas. If you've never been much of an artist, it is execution—not creativity—with which you need help. The landscape painter's perspective is creative; the brushstrokes are execution of the creative vision. Failing to recognize the difference—especially in the realm of presentations—can have serious consequences. If you have a creative vision, you can find a way to execute it. But if you have no vision, your presentation will surely suffer.

Remember, creativity requires confidence above all else. So it's no coincidence that excellent presentations depend upon confidence as well. When we hesitate to put our best ideas forward and instead invite others to step in and do the thinking for us, we commit a grievous sin against the presentation we will give. It is *our* message. *We* are responsible for the results and consequences of what is said on stage. After all, great coaches don't outsource the training and then show up for the big game; they become great by leading excellent training programs. Your presentation is the same: You have a responsibility to be intimately involved with both its construction and design.

Now, if you lack artistic skills, it is always a good idea to outsource the execution to someone who can bring your creativity to life. Whereas everyone is truly creative, not everyone is proficient with advanced design software or current design trends. We need to separate creativity and execution because our message is our baby—it doesn't makes sense to let someone else raise it—but our vision is not complete without skill.

So how do we engage our inner creative beast? If we're no longer passing the creative buck, how do we envision and communicate our creative ideas to the people who need to catch our message most? Like many of you, my professional career has required me to rehabilitate my creative mind. In the process, I've identified some perspectives and strategies that are extremely helpful when tasked with plucking intangible thoughts out of my brain and putting them into a roomful of audience members' hearts.

Seek Deeply, Seek Widely

Imitation is the most sincere form of flattery. If you've ever heard a great musician interviewed, you know that this is true. Inevitably, they nod their heads to the musicians they admired growing up and, most of the time, you can hear faint traces of those influences in the music they make.

Humans are expert parrots. Our brains ingest a profound amount of data during almost every moment of every day. As we walk around living our lives, we're passing influence after influence that is fair game for use in our presentations; yet we oftentimes discount these influences for any number of reasons—too easy, too edgy, "it's not me," and yes, "I'm not creative like that." Presenting

Humans
ARE
EXPERT
parrots.

is an out-of-body experience, a notion we touched upon earlier. To that end, the simple act of stepping on stage predisposes the audience to think of you as an authority figure. Embrace this fact for the freedom it awards you! You get the chance to become completely dissociated from all of your preconceived notions of yourself when you give a presentation. It's an opportunity to be different, bolder, and more enlivened than the "you" in your daily life. You can take risks for a simple reason: You're on stage, and they are not. Regardless of content, design, or delivery, the worst presentations are the safe ones. They are boring. And they stink.

So open your horizons. Seek both deeply and widely, to discover new and effective ways of reaching your audience. Every movie you watch, story you read, and billboard or advertisement you see can inform your approach for the next presentation. If something affects you, analyze it: What causes that reaction within you? Are the colors strangely appealing? Does the text pop out at you? Do you identify with the scene being presented or with the implied theme of a particular image? Whatever the case, introspection can allow you to become a homegrown expert on outstanding design. And if I haven't said it yet, I'll say it now: design is very, very important in your presentation. It's on equal ground with both content and delivery. You cannot create great presentations without paying attention to design.

Talk to Strangers

Let me clarify: If an El Camino pulls up next to you and the driver offers you a Snickers bar, you should still run away. But unmarked vans and candy-toting creeps aside, it's time to shelve your mother's childhood warnings. In the professional world, new experiences with different types of people can be immensely helpful, especially when attempting to reach a large group of (let's be honest) complete strangers during a presentation.

Most likely, you are not a member of your target audience. If you were, you'd know exactly what you needed to see and hear to make the decision you wanted yourself to make. I'm sure some of us could find a way to complicate it, but for the most part, convincing ourselves to do what we want is a fairly easy assignment. Similarly, your close-knit group of friends is likely to be only slightly broader than your own personality. It's human nature to prefer our comfort zones, find our circles of trust, and ride them out until we're all shuffling around nursing homes together. But it's terrible for business, especially in terms of mass communication.

If you want to be able to step out of the box and start understanding what other people like and respond to, you've got to start collecting personalities like bottle caps or baseball cards. (Note: Please don't expressly state that you are "gathering specimens" during your reconnaissance. That approach has a way of morbidly terrifying your new friends.) Presentation design is a pragmatic art. The final look and feel of the presentation exists to please the audience, not the speaker. Thus, the onus is on you to understand what your particular audience is likely to embrace. The only way to do that effectively is to establish relational resources that you can exploit from time to time for assistance. After all, you can spend all day trying to channel a mid-level mortgage broker's innermost desires, or you can call a few mid-level mortgage brokers themselves and ask them whatever you want. Start building a network of strangers-turned-acquaintances so that your presentation design can dial in a little more specifically. Just knowing that your mid-level mortgage broker's favorite brands are Rolex, BMW, and Sobe gives you a tremendous head start on the design direction of your entire presentation.

Fail Often and Like It

Those idiot colonial explorers thought the world was flat—literally, a sheet of world! Obviously, some of them doubted the geography of the day enough to get on a boat and head for the edge anyway, but have you ever wondered: What if it really had been flat? They would have sailed right off the edge, apparently into the mouth of a massive saltwater-drinking serpent of some sort, if we were to believe the creative mapmakers of the day.

And then, of course, there were the more reliable setbacks of scurvy, mutiny, shipwrecks, squalls, starvation, and piracy. In fact, you might reasonably conclude that the aspiration to discover new lands was tantamount to suicide.

The result? Names etched in the collective memory of human civilization. That's all.

If we want to really achieve, we have to reconcile ourselves to the likelihood of failure. We also need to understand an extremely important fact about failure: There is nothing permanent about it. Read any biography or memoir of an important human in history, and you'll discover that roughly one-third to half of the book essentially chronicles the repeated failures that led to their success. When you sail into the unknown you'll sometimes find

PUSH

YOUR DESIGN TO THE *edge* OF STATUS QUO,

hold your nose,

& JUMP.

the edge of the world. Other times, you'll strike pure gold. The only way to miss out on the positive is to never leave the harbor.

So acquire a taste for failure. Reach extremely high. Push your design to the edge of status quo, hold your nose, and jump.

You may miss or there may be a giant serpent that gobbles you up at the bottom. But who cares? Far more dangerous than failure is delivering a routine presentation; these are the ones we're all looking out for and desperately trying to avoid. Routine presentations are boring. They're depressing. They're forgotten. And you know what? They don't garner better results than your colossal failure, anyway.

Think about the YouTube videos you watch: do you lean toward monotone book reports on Robinson Crusoe, or do you watch some wild and crazy child reenacting the story with Barbie dolls? You may not be inclined to follow the crazy, delusional child, but you'll at least have had a laugh or two. You may even buy the book.

This is what we're going for with our presentations. We're getting their attention, extending our hands as far out as we can to touch the audience. Great presentation design begins with great presentation philosophy: If you set out to make an impression and put reservations and insecurities aside for the glory of what may be, you'll come away with something, even if the presentation is a total failure—a good story, a reputation for being daring, or a sort of primal respect from the audience because they could never get up on stage and try to fly the way you did.

The pursuit is what makes us great, not the results, though being great almost certainly guarantees results at some point.

Sometimes your throw is a last-second Hail Mary into the end zone; other times, it is a hand grenade that blows up in your face. Don't cry when this happens. Just shovel the dirt back into the crater and start again.

Keep Dreaming

The more you practice creativity, the more you'll find that it is an approach to life, not a means to a great presentation. Living creatively has benefits far beyond PowerPoint and projectors: it is helpful in marriage, with children, even in understanding yourself and growing as a person. Turning it off, insofar as one is able, is like choosing black and white after seeing color. Why would you ever do that?

My own pursuit of dynamic thinking has led me to make a surprising discovery: creativity is energizing, not exhausting. In fact, I've realized over time that the routine, the status quo, and the boring are far more draining than bright and exuberant living. Settling down may sound like maturity, but in reality it's a short ride to the grave. The mind craves experience. So start overeating.

SHOPTALK: PRESENTATION DESIGN STYLES AND APPROACHES

Jazz musicians have their scales; artists have figure drawing; and writers have grammar. Every creative outlet has parameters that guide expression. It's how we keep our heads from popping off. The difference between a toddler whacking a pot with a spoon and a jazz drummer riffing through syncopated rhythms is an understanding of fundamental rules. Such is the difference between a beatnik art house monologue and a stellar presentation.

Garr Reynolds first introduced me (and many others) to the world's leading presentation styles in his landmark blog and book, *Presentation Zen*. I have been studying and following the preeminent presentation design methods in the world ever since. Even more, I've been employing them in my own presentations and hearing feedback from others. Undoubtedly, everyone will respond to one method more than another; however, we need to consider these methods like gambling in baseball. You may be a diehard Red Sox fan, but are you really going to put your money on them against the Yankees? I mean, you've got to put food on the table.

Okay, so now that I've lost the respect of all Bostonians, let's take a look at the prevailing approaches of our time.

The Godin Method

The Godin Method, named after the illustrious Seth Godin, is based on a hilariously simple concept: The art of presenting is actually composed of two different elements, the speaker and the slide. Mind-blowing, huh?

Actually, it is. The speaker, as the name suggests, speaks. Speakers use words. They are the experts whose thoughts everyone has gathered to hear on the matter at hand. With that in mind, doesn't it strike you as oddly repetitive to plaster slides with words, sentences, and even paragraphs? After all, do you want the audience to listen or to read? Have you ever tried doing both at the same time?

Of course, no speaker wants the audience to read. Why not just mail them pamphlets and save everyone the trouble of gathering in the first place? No, we give presentations because we understand, on some level, that words by themselves are insufficient to communicate the material.

Then we have the slides. Everyone knows a picture is worth a thousand words. Imagine the number of memories you create just by looking at a photograph of a barn. You could be transported to the old family farm, to childhood, to vacations with your children when they were young. These memories, in turn, generate a tempest of feeling, from joy to pain to somber reflection and back again.

Yes, a picture is worth a thousand words. But which words? Without the separate, complementary presence of a speaker, pictures are nothing more than random associations. This is fine if your ultimate purpose is to simply elicit feelings from the audience, but it is grossly insufficient if you are tasked with moving them to action based on those feelings. Artfully weaving the strength of the presenter's presence with the raw power of slide imagery is what makes the Godin method so utterly effective. So how does one employ it?

Remember: You are an expert. All of the neurons inside your head are connected just right, helping you understand your particular area of expertise. But the neurons of your audience aren't situated for that information, and your job is to get them there in the span of a 45-minute keynote. The slide images, as used in the Godin method, are your trusty sidekicks. They allow you to focus on deep, meaningful content without scorching your audience's cerebellums.

Let's put it this way: You're giving an in-depth talk on the underlying neurological processes that govern how grief is navigated. You can put bullet points on each slide that repeat exactly what you just said, or you can utilize deeply personal images of denial, guilt, anger, and so on. Analogous and poignant imagery entertains the audience in a way that projected sentences cannot. Far from being distracting, entertaining imagery actually keeps the audience alert and in a state that facilitates learning and engagement.

The Takahashi Method

For Masayoshi Takahashi, slides are like the breadcrumbs in *Hansel and Gretel*: They mark a path for the audience. Takahashi stumbled upon his technique when confronted with what, for many of us, would be an absolute nightmare: a presentation opportunity without our precious slide decks, editing software, or advanced technology. Yet by rolling the dice on a startling assumption about the human brain, he won big.

Takahashi approached the presentation with the simple belief that his audience would have an open mind and a basic willingness to engage—so long as he didn't get in the way of his story. For each slide, he distilled his key points down to a single, powerful word. He told the story and let the bold, raw power of each single word emblazon his message into the minds of the audience members. No glitz, no glamour: just a powerful message with a roadmap the audience could follow.

The Takahashi method is not so different from the Godin method. After all, where do we cross the line between pictures and words? When we're young, letters are just primitive figures on a page. Only later do we become desensitized to the word as imagery. But by isolating key words and displaying them with sovereign weight on the projection screen, we access that primal sense of words as art.

Think about a word like "breathe." We breathe every day—nothing new there. Yet within the context of a presentation on stress relief at work, with the lights set low, that single, suddenly odd-sounding word—*breathe*—develops layers. What does it mean to breathe? When are we ever conscious of breathing? When our kids are born? When we're afraid? When we're physically exhausted? The more we contemplate the underground life of even the most pedestrian words, the more we encounter our own introspective natures. When I set out to teach a group of people something dynamic and new, that's the headspace where I want to put them.

The Lessig Method

Like Godin and Takahashi, Lawrence Lessig considers the slide deck to be supplementary to the speaker's personal expertise. The slides are a lifeline between the audience and your content: They can visually hold on to your thought process as you bumble down the road.

Unlike Godin and Takahashi, however, Lessig isn't focused on whether imagery or stark words are superior. His method combines the two and instead focuses on brevity and slide volume throughout. Rather than boiling all of your content down to a key word (as with the Takahashi method) or an image (the Godin method), Lessig ratchets up the slide count so that each concept has multiple slides that batter the point home. In fact, I've seen Lessig deliver 20- to 30-minute presentations that had over 200 slides. It's almost like watching a narrated flip-book.

The logic behind the method is simple: Think back to how you learned the alphabet, or how you taught your kids. The letter *A* is presented both as a word, Apple, and as an image of an apple. *B* is for Book, and an image is there for visual reference. Humans are meaning machines—a bad maize harvest in the Mayan empire inevitably produced a corresponding angry maize god—and we perform our vast calculations rapidly to whatever end we're given. Lessig became a master at making the meaning-machine mind work for him. Every concept is broken up into the fundamental parts and then represented in slide form with a key word, image, or both. Every slide in this method is perfectly clear, because every concept is perfectly reduced to bite-size form.

The Lessig method also gives the audience a feeling of rapid transit. Moving through 20 to 30 slides a minute, with each slide in perfect synchronization with a prepared and rehearsed narrative, makes it exceedingly difficult to look away—even if you're not particularly interested in the subject matter. You get the sense that you could miss volumes of information in the space of a few seconds, and the slides change so often that you don't have time to get bored.

This method has its limitations—an hour-long keynote could approach 500 slides, creating a budgetary and logistical nightmare—and requires some dedicated preparation. Timing is more than just a personal touch here; it is crucial to the delivery and is as much a part of the presentation's success as the content or design. If you run out of time with your rapid-fire succession of slides, you'll look more like a drunk groomsman giving an unfortunate toast than a seasoned expert with valuable information to share with an eager audience.

The Kawasaki Method

Guy Kawasaki, venture capital phenom and honorary presentation god, has a method that has as its central tenet a concept we discussed earlier: don't ruin their day. His 10/20/30 Rule—10 slides per presentation, 20 minutes for delivery, and 30-point fonts—addresses some of the fundamental errors that plague most presenters today. Ten slides may seem grossly insufficient for your complex content, but Kawasaki raises the question: If you can't boil it down to that, how clearly do you *really* understand it? Likewise, approaching your 45-minute paid keynote slot with 20 minutes of material could come off as offensive to the group that signs your check, and 30-point fonts are pretty large, right?

But as Kawasaki is quick to bring up, what if it takes you 15 minutes to set up your computer? What if one key decision maker arrives 10 minutes late and the other has to leave 20 minutes early? And the more you speak to C-level executives, the more you need those big fonts, because with wisdom and experience come myopia and cataracts.

Every presenter needs to be thoroughly proficient with a Kawasaki-esque presentation; however, not every presentation lends itself to this method. This approach is your best shot when you have to give a big pitch to a busy, cut-the-bull decider who wants all of the pertinent information and none of the snap, crackle, or pop. Design these presentations with clarity and legibility as priority guideposts. Aesthetics won't be as important for the sort of audience you're speaking to when dealing in Kawasakis.

Pecha Kucha

As haikus or sonnets are to the written word, Pecha Kucha is to the presentation. Pecha Kucha is a rigid prescription for slide and content structure—just 20 slides shown for 20 seconds per slide. If you want to do 23 slides, or spend 30 seconds on each slide, that's fine. But it's not Pecha Kucha.

If you feel as though we've suddenly exited the realm of meaningful information and entered a disturbing, but ultimately harmless, attic apartment where presentation geeks make up arbitrary rules about information delivery, then this will erase any remaining doubt: Pecha Kucha nights, where individuals gather to brandish their brevity skills before peers, actually take place all over the world. There are no business contracts to snag at these forums and no political agendas to push. They are just presentations for the love of the game, the way you might have played pickup basketball as a kid.

Before you put down the book and start searching YouTube for your next viral Facebook post, let me explain. Pecha Kucha may not be fundamentally relevant for your presentation, but there is a lot to be gained by using this method during your training and practice. I cannot emphasize this point enough: when presenting, clarity and brevity are paramount. Nothing clutters the mind more than useless words, cumbersome sentences, and stumbling monologues. No one is going to force you to don a Darth Vader mask and attend your local Pecha Kucha night, but please consider putting strict limitations on your slide count and minutes/seconds per slide. Sometimes we can't find a better way to say something until we're faced with a time limit and have to cut. Pecha Kucha is a great practice method, and it really does help me eliminate previously unseen superfluity, no matter what approach I choose for my final deck.

Ignite

Now that you're a diehard Pecha Kucha night attendee, I have some bad news for you. There are others out there. In particular, a group called Ignite has disciples who scoff at your luxuriously long-winded 20 seconds per slide. These Spartan speakers are doing it in 15 seconds, and if that sounds like a trivial difference, just get out the stopwatch: Read a sentence that takes 20 seconds to complete, and try to pare it down to a comfortably articulated 15 seconds while retaining all of the important information. Ignite presentations force the brain to work the language like a crossword puzzle, finding all the possible permutations available to settle on information that is almost mathematically selected.

Yes, there are Ignite nights as well. Yes, I know you categorically refuse to attend. If you take anything away from these final two methods, make it brevity. Both of these methods are like lifting weights in a gym so that you can build a cabin out of logs. They're imitations of a truer purpose, sure, but they can certainly make you strong.

THE TAKEAWAY

Obviously, these methods are not exactly universal in their applicability. Takahashi is intense and introspective; Kawasaki is business-brief. Lessig spoon-feeds conceptual bites, effectively brainwashing entire audiences with a slide progression that sidesteps the rational mind; Godin painstakingly selects images that pull on heartstrings, opens old wounds, and manipulates the subconscious into overt acceptance of whatever wordless message is being conveyed.

Most of us aren't presenting at seminars on presenting or teaching academic courses on mass communication. Most of us are out there in the real world, getting support or money or clients in order to feed our families and better society. There's no room for making our content an experiment in presentation trends, but each method underscores a key aspiration for the real-life presentations we're delivering. You'll notice, across the board, that every method makes an attempt to eliminate the hot air and get straight to the point. What does that lead us to think about the purpose of design in our presentations? We want it clear. We want it concise. We want it to blend very neatly with our narrative so that each complements the other. Most of all, we want design to keep the audience close by and alert.

With these goals in mind, it's time to get down and dirty with design.

Chapter 9

Real Simple

Your message is like a flock of beautiful white doves. As you organize and prepare for the big day, you feed and coddle your doves with doting commitment, as though you were the mother dove. You pour your heart and soul into these innocent birds, whose stark white plumage and gentle cooing seems to personify the ideals of peace, hope, and love. When you watch them take flight, you feel transported to a metaphysical land where mortgages, sales quotas, and third-quarter projections lie in calm docility beside your bank account. Happiness and harmony are there.

Doves, however, are considered by many to be the rats of the aviary world—right next to pigeons, the possums of the same. A flock of garbling, pigment-less flying rats swooping through the air calls to mind bird crap and avian flu—not peace, hope, and love—to these practical realists. That's *your* message I'm talking about.

What happens when you set your message loose over an audience? Does the audience swat at the dumpy projectiles, or do they outstretch their arms, hands, and fingers as perches for worthy inspiration?

In other words: How do we control what our message is once we surrender control and give it to others?

LESS REALLY *IS* MORE

We talk a lot about trust in presentations: how to build it, how to maintain it, how to leverage that trust into millions of dollars in slush funds for our personal pleasure, and so on. But we rarely look at trust from an equally valid angle: How can you trust your audience?

If you've never thought about this before, you should. When we stand behind the dais and look out across a sea (or puddle, depending on the situation) of faces, we're at an even greater disadvantage than the audience. Forget superficial character judgments; we don't even have time to verify they're not all blow-up dolls. Most of us hop up on stage and get straight to talking, never vetting the audience for the capacity to steward a message that, as aforementioned, is as precious as our flock of nirvana-doves.

This may sound audacious, but how important is your message? Is it nuanced? Are there gray areas, or intangibles that the audience must sense rather than see? So often, the potency of our content is wrapped up in our own unique perspective and understanding of the issue(s) at hand. Are you willing to take that nuanced message and put it in the hands of the scrubby-looking guy in the back with crooked sideburns and his shirt tucked into his underwear? What if he's the southeastern regional representative for your company? How confident can you be that he's getting the full measure of passion and drive that you're putting out there regarding the new product line?

What's worse about untrustworthy audiences (or individual members thereof) is that we presenters are still responsible for what they do with our message once they leave the room. If they snatch a white dove in the air but trip, fall, and crush it, guess what: you're still the white dove guy, and it's your fault. So what can we do to prevent failure due to incompetent, disinterested, or lazy attendees?

For starters, keep it simple—really, really simple. The thing about sharp go-getters is that they're sharp go-getters; they hold eco-friendly nets over the birdcage and rush off with as many white doves as they can in order to breed and share them with the world. I'm not telling you to ignore them; I'm just saying that the portion of the audience that will take your message and run with it will do so regardless of its simplicity.

No, our task is to reach the skeptics, the dimly lit, the recalcitrant, or the argumentative. This is aiming for the stars and hitting the moon: If we craft our presentations for the toughest audience members, we're bound to cover our bases with everyone else.

This is precisely why simplicity is king. The message should be inspirational to the catatonic; understandable to the dumb (sorry); legible to the illiterate; and logical to the crazy.

In the previous chapter, we covered the prevailing design styles of our time. Images, very few words, minimal information,

THE MESSAGE SHOULD BE

inspirational
TO THE **CATATONIC;**

understandable
TO THE **DUMB (sorry);**

legible
TO THE **ILLITERATE;**

&

logical
TO THE **CRAZY.**

and story-like flow characterize these styles, and they should characterize your presentation as well. Think children's picture books for adults.

This doesn't mean your message has to be humble or earthly. We should never confuse simplicity in presentation design for overall simplicity; after all, some of us are going to be using these presentations to usher in never-before-seen technological advances or unprecedented new world orders. Some of you may be trying to take over the world, for all I know. That's complicated stuff, but we can still find a way to explain ourselves clearly and directly.

So, for the design illiterate, what criteria are we using for aesthetic simplicity?

Detox Design

Humans have a strong tribal instinct: We want to understand and be understood by others. I see countless presentations each year where the speaker's pursuit of equal-plane comprehension—that is, bringing the audience *completely* up to speed on his or her knowledge—effectively sabotages the entire presentation. Indeed, the first step to clean, efficient design is to identify areas that *don't* need to be covered. If your objective is to solidify third-party funding for a new land development project, how relevant is a listing of problems and hurdles you've faced along the way? Or even an inspiring history of the land prior to your development plan? The third party wants to know one thing: will we get our money back? Will there be a return on our investment? Detox. Detox. Detox.

Detoxing design is the same as detoxing content. Keep your ultimate objective very close at hand, and read it out loud as you examine each slide. Ask yourself: does this slide have any information or imagery that does *not* immediately serve my objective? I find this question to be a valuable gut check. On many occasions, I've seen it eliminate vast amounts of confusing or tangential information that might have prevented a thorough understanding of the concepts being communicated to the audience.

I always detox my presentations before doing anything else. First, it's practical: Why invest time or money designing slides that are going to be scrapped, pared down, or altered significantly? Though I always plan for revisions, do-overs can kill. Second, the detoxing process—which is really a thorough, post-content editing job that dictates design—gives me insight as to the look and feel I'm going for. The more you interact with your message (editing and removing, changing and modifying, revisiting and explaining), the more you develop a sort of intimate connection with what your presentation is, and what it is not—bold or beautiful, hip or classic, geek or hunk, and so on.

Shun ambiguity. Be easily deciphered. Detox your design.

Design You'd Take Home to Mom

If you've ever brought someone you just met to a family wedding, you've hopefully learned this lesson well: Impulsivity makes for great memoirs later in life, but lots of humiliation in the present moment. You need at least one night—preferably more—to think and *re*think your design scheme. Falling in love is one thing; making a commitment is entirely another.

Obviously, no one is going to revoke a contract because you presented with a mullet in the 1980s—we're not talking about forecasting trends and avoiding the long arm of history here. What we're talking about is a short, two- or three-day buffer zone between the *Incredible Hulk* comp image you started with and the mountaintop comp on which you truly should be settling for the upcoming Series A Finance Campaign. When you mastered the art of creativity, you developed a valuable skill: fearlessness. This buffer zone is your first line of defense against one of the unfortunate side effects of fearlessness: stupidity.

2D Thin

3D may be all the rage these days, but a 3D concept is a forgotten concept. Think about Super Mario: Once upon a time, we only had to focus on up and down, left and right. These days, it's a veritable nightmare trying to get the tubby Italian to do anything other than run in circles. Sure, Millennials could probably do it, but chances are they're not the ones signing off on the big deal you're trying to close.

2D equals concise. Don't add unnecessary layers or images. If you can portray something more directly, do so. When it comes to audience attention spans, the sum is definitely not equal to the parts. Thin decks are powerful decks when they're thin because of thorough planning and revisions. Just don't take this advice as the go ahead to procrastinate and throw a three-slide deck together a few minutes before the big talk. That won't go over well—I promise.

Sure, there is such a thing as *too* thin. Today's supermodels can't board a plane without TSA officials confiscating their razor-sharp knees and elbows. So don't get carried away. But at the end of the day, we want thin. Modern laptops are so thin they're capable of inflicting surgical incisions on our wrists while we type, but who cares? They look so good. And that is exactly what the audience will be thinking as you sear their minds with a razor-thin deck that complements your authoritative voice with precisely chosen imagery. Give them just enough data and information to help them sign on the dotted line. 3D is great for action films, but few of us have the blue skin and Navi instincts of *Avatar* to make a 3D presentation sizzle.

Design 101

Now that we've established some of the overarching quality control concerns pertaining to design, we're faced with the question most of us fear the most: How am *I* going to design a presentation? While most of us have moved on from Prodigy Internet and the cd-space file execution of Microsoft DOS, very few of us have kept pace with the frenetic development of today's artistic software. The good news for all of us is that the principles of good design apply to any skill level.

Many presentations more than justify the expense of enlisting a designer or specialty firm to build a presentation from the ground up that will be so hot it curls the eyelashes. But others don't. For example, a glossy presentation designed by a boutique firm might not be the best approach for a downsizing forum. (You may want to leave the Rolex at home, too.) In reality, design in the presentation realm is function first, form second. You can nail the first by employing solid design principles; the second, if you can afford it, will certainly help.

The bad news, then, is that no one is off the hook: If you choose to walk in with some lame, bullet-pointed, and Excel-charted visual catastrophe, you will be condemned. There's no Age of Accountability doctrine, either. You've been warned, and any bullet points—or the use of that ovular clip art shadow man pre-installed on every Windows operating system, for that matter—will cause you to writhe in a tortuous hall of eternal presentation failures. In a painful twist of the age-old public speaking trick, you'll be the naked one and everyone else will have clothes on for all eternity. In this personal terror, you will always speak on the same topics: why calculus matters and why you talk to your mother that way. It will be awkward—painfully so.

Dante may have failed to mention the fate of people who give bad presentations, but there you have it. Here are some basic guidelines that, if followed, will at least get you into purgatory, if not delivering keynotes with St. Peter on reasonable metrics regarding the pleasant fluffiness of heaven's clouds.

FONTS

1. Bigger is better. Guy Kawasaki's guideline—30-point fonts or bigger—is a good one to follow, even if you have more than 10 slides or speak longer than 20 minutes.
2. Fonts should never blend in with a background or image.
3. Fancy = illegible, especially from the back of the room. Keep it simple, people.

   For instance:
   Schoolhouse Cursive tells an audience, "Since the day I was born, it has been important to me that none of my ideas are understood."

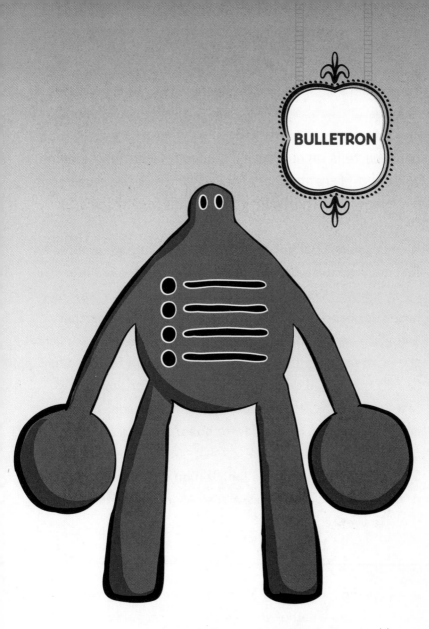

BULLETRON

*Bullet points are like bullets —
they kill people. It's the weapon of
choice for **Bulletron**.*

You should also be wary of stigmatic fonts, like Comic Sans or Papyrus:

Papyrus tells an audience, "I have an insatiable desire to feel different. Therefore, I write in the same font everyone else that wants to feel different uses."

4. Be polygamous but never promiscuous. Using two or three fonts throughout a presentation provides a nice break in style; using more makes you look like a preschooler with crayons.

5. Lose your heart in Sans Serif. Serifs are the little tails that embellish certain fonts. Sans serif fonts, as the name explicitly states, have no serifs. Generally speaking, serif fonts are for heavily text-based documents; sans serif is for simple, low-text applications. Pop question: should your slides have lots and lots of words, or very few to none? Answer: sans serif for presentations.

6. STOP YELLING. Wanton capitalization isn't nice. Use italics or larger fonts for emphasis; all-caps phrases make audiences feel like they're in trouble.

NUMBERS

1. Enhance their self-image. The statisticians in the crowd will track with you whether you use clearly designed charts and graphs or just rattle off complex equations that make what you say true. Since no one else can track with the latter, use the charts and graphs, and keep them explicitly clear and well labeled.

2. Keep them grounded. Perspective—that elusive and changeable aspect of vision that makes raw input meaningful

to the human mind—depends upon comparison. We can fathom the heft of 2.5 tons by picturing a Dodge Ram. Balancing quantitative data with qualitative analogies prevents the sort of spontaneous narcolepsy known to infect vast audiences during the more technical elements of a presentation.

3. Use a spoonful of sugar. Data, like medicine, is often a bitter pill to swallow. Data also tends to isolate the analytical side of the brain, which happens to be the less emotional side and therefore less responsive to themes. You can engage both the analytical and creative parts of the brain by combining data and imagery, a visual concoction known as infographics. Let's say you're presenting on nutrition trends in America: using infographics is as simple as replacing those dreary bar graphs with proportional segments of candy bars. All infographics should be rather literal in their translation from graphic to data; otherwise, you're just creating additional mind-work for the audience.

4. Wham! Data should be the final, decisive point on a well-developed argument. Think of numbers as a sort of trump card, like the ace of spades, that you slap down on the table to seal the deal. Littering numbers here and there throughout the presentation diffuses their impact, whereas saving them for crucial closing statements can provide the final push for a truly action-inducing finale.

Imagery

While I encourage every presenter to engage in creative expression, I do have to qualify this exhortation: Endless tinkering with background colors and patterns should be expressly avoided.

MR.

HEAVY
PANTS

*There is nothing good about
data heavy presentations
unless you want to look like*
Mr. Heavy Pants.

Serial manipulation of these aspects of your presentation does more to suggest idle playtime than concept or theme advancement. And of all the qualities you want to display during a presentation, idleness is one that surely falls to the bottom of the list.

Furthermore, we must move beyond the curiously persistent use of the Windows clip art character in presentations all around the globe: Screen Bean, who is always hitting his constantly crashing Microsoft product with a sledgehammer. This brand of clip art behavior, like many of the things that happened during fraternity pledge week, should be buried deep in the past. So what if you ate a family-sized jar of mayonnaise to make some friends? No one cares, as long as you've moved on from that sort of stunt-based relationship building and left it in the distant, distant past. Unfortunately, it just doesn't translate to conference rooms or board meetings. Otherwise, the world's wealthiest would be a different breed, indeed. To that end, Screen Bean—like the consumption of whole jars of condiments—won't ruin you so long as you never, ever speak to him again. You wouldn't wear a clip-on tie to a presentation; why would you use clip art?

So without Screen Bean or the many-faceted stock backgrounds that accompany PowerPoint these days, what does one present to the public? The answer is not photos from your personal family albums or a diabolical mind-control scheme. You probably make weird faces in most of the pictures, not to mention the uncomfortable revelation of odd family rituals, and, pertaining to the latter, you are most likely not a Jedi knight. Instead, stock photography is the ideal approach. Online databases are searchable and vast, generally having more than enough options to suit your needs.

You get what you pay for with stock photography. The famed Getty Images provide the widest array of seriously artful images for the presentation where a truly aesthetic veneer is necessary. However, you can get by on the cheap if you need to. Affordable options like iStockphoto.com or Fotolia.com offer a wide range of imagery in the $1 to $3 per photo price range. One thing I really enjoy about paying for imagery is the peace of mind that comes with the purchase. I know I'm not infringing on copyrights and can feel confident that I'm not exposing myself to liabilities during a presentation.

At the end of the day, though, I know that many of you just refuse to pay for imagery. There are a few ways you can minimize or eliminate copyright infringement liability and still use compelling photos in your presentations. Google is great for breadth, but good quality can be hard to find, and you'll have to dig to find out whether or not you have the right to use any images you find. Flickr.com recently launched a service that allows access to photos that have what is called a Creative Commons license—basically, you can use them for free. The site is a public forum for both amateur and professional photography, but you'd be surprised at how talented some of these amateurs really are. It may take some legwork to find the right image, but there's always going to be some form of sacrifice when you're not paying.

Other, similar resources include free stock photo sites like Publicdomainpictures.com and Everystockphoto.com.

Additionally, the U. S. National Archive has a database of stock photos that are free for public use at Archive.org. The latter is a great way to start enjoying the exclusive member benefits you receive when paying your annual dues to Uncle Sam's club. You can add all of these sites to a bookmarks bar for quick and easy access when the next presentation project arrives.

The Rule of Thirds

The Rule of Thirds is easier seen than read, so try this out: Visit any professional photography site and rifle through some of their images. You may notice that few, if any, of the photographs place their primary focus directly in the center of the picture or at the fringes. This is the Rule of Thirds at work: Imagine that these photographs are divided into thirds both vertically and horizontally. You end up with a grid of nine squares (something like the intro to *The Brady Bunch*). Imagery that positions the object(s) of interest along these lines, or at the intersection of these lines (the four corners of the center square), is considered to be more interesting than imagery where the subject is exactly centered.

Obviously, with rules come rule breakers. However, the vast majority of us are not attempting to usher in new eras of artistic expression with our presentations; we're just trying to reach an audience. Using the Rule of Thirds can really simplify the do-it-yourself design process for most of us by providing some literal guidelines along which we can place our images with confidence.

Hope for the Hopeless

Though I find it increasingly difficult to keep in touch with them, I do know a few individuals who are immensely successful but have a crazy person's mistrust of electronic gadgetry. Obviously, budgets and skills are not going to be the only barriers between such old school stalwarts and the Most Innovative Presentation of 2011 award. Nevertheless, even the most prehistoric presenter can deliver a stunning presentation with somewhat primitive devices.

Perhaps one of the best examples of primitive presenting in the modern age is comedian Demetri Martin. Though one of those technology-saturated Millennials, Martin frequently employs flip charts, chalkboards, or whiteboards as part of his comedic routine. This conceit is clearly effective, promoting a sort of professorial intimacy between speaker and audience that draws upon the school-age familiarity of the chalkboard lecture. There is certainly an opportunity for individuals to capture and own this presentation style, especially as more and more presentations cross over into the digital realm, becoming the status quo. Digital is always going to be easier, but if you're really uncomfortable with technology, you can still deliver a stellar presentation by mastering the flip chart technique.

Spread the Love

One final option for the technologically inept would be to farm your presentation out. Don't take it overseas, though; give a college student the once-in-a-lifetime opportunity to work with a first-class presenter and professional. Local art schools or design departments at major universities will likely have many students who are desperate for internships and professional experience. If you can't hire professionals but don't have the time or heart to bring your presentation design up to date, let a cost-effective intern take a stab at it. Tomorrow's high-priced design experts are in school today. They need experience; you need help. Why not give each other a shot?

What's the Gist?

You can get a Ph.D. in Graphic Design. In fact, the Ph.D.s can get even more specific than that. Visual communication is an art, but there is science involved as well. So let yourself off the hook: If you're going to be good at your own job, at some point you have to give up being an expert on everything else. Occasionally, this means that your time is better off spent focusing on your area of expertise and paying someone else to focus on theirs—designing your presentations. Other times, strict budgets just won't allow it. This cursory overview of suitable design tactics should arm you with enough information to either articulate what you want to a presentation design expert or put your best foot forward and far surpass any presentation in which Screen Bean makes an appearance.

Chapter 10

Parting the Clouds

Me? I like sitting at home on Saturdays trying to figure out how to make a PowerPoint 2007 file convert to a laptop that only has Keynote 2009. I think of it as technological skydiving, mainly because it makes the hair on the back of my neck stand up and because, if I am unsuccessful in my endeavor, every bone in my professional body will be pulverized into a fine powder. That sort of primal fear is fun to me; it's like playing Clue with a friend who actually is a killer.

Since I'm writing for a larger audience, though, I have to assume that at least a small percentage of you don't enjoy occupational Russian roulette, and might not get any sort of sadistic pleasure out of arriving at a presentation venue only to discover that the projector is not compatible with your computer and you'll have to use the archaic house system that lacks any sort of file management or conversion capability. The thing about "planning ahead" is that we usually learn to do it only once we've been burned, badly. That first time is always a doozy. When the inevitable happens, you hopefully have a flipchart and one of those fist-sized markers that lets you write in 60-point font. Otherwise, you may want to encourage all decision makers to huddle up at your feet.

PowerPoint has been the de facto presentation design software since it debuted in 1987. For many years, the primary advantage it had over potential competitors was that it merely existed. Keynote 1.0 debuted in 2003, just 16 years later. Other programs have come and gone, but these two enjoy the sort of rich market suffusion that only the most successful technology companies in the world can provide. Sure, there've been problems over the years: The templates are boring, the capabilities are not ambitious, the vintage years don't sync well, the display is sometimes indescribably awry, and the programs—especially PowerPoint—seem to occasionally crash just for fun. But both have been good to some people some of the time. And really, what more can we ask for?

Evidently, a lot: hordes of revolutionaries are taking their business, or at least their presentation design, to the grid. It will no doubt come as a surprise for many that other options actually do exist. This is sort of like trying to discover where you are going to Google something if not at Google. Remember: we're giving presentations here, not PowerPoints or Keynotes. Well, maybe we're giving keynotes, but just this once let's not fall victim to Steve Jobs' marketing savvy.

The truth is that PowerPoint and Keynote have existed in false competition with one another for decades simply because of their ubiquity, a quality that has more to do with their honorary positions in the Microsoft Office and Apple iWork suites of software (respectively) than with any sort of inherent virtues. Slide design and content organization should be simple to begin with, so we're really not looking for programs that have some sort

of magical thought-converting algorithms that take harebrained ideas and turn them into multimillion-dollar patented inventions. No, what we really want is seamless convertibility and crisis avoidance technology. We're simply trying to show up at a venue without the cycle of fear touchy programming instills.

You might get the impression that I'm anti-PowerPoint and anti-Keynote. Far from it: In my capacity as CEO of presentation design company Ethos3, I utilize both programs on a daily basis. Quirks and frustrations aside, these programs do allow the habitual presenter to produce meaningful slide decks every day. They're standard on most computers, which sets my heart somewhat at ease, since it ensures that presentations are not being designed with the spray paint feature in Microsoft Paint—or worse, with bullet points in 60-point font on Word documents.

But competition is ultimately good for us—the little revolutionaries seeking to take over the planet with our world-changing Pez dispenser modifications and the hopes for distribution that go along with them, or whatever other crazy ideas we might have. New presentation design applications that have the potential to improve presentation design for the common man are cropping up—a development that should have serious ramifications in Pez after-markets around the world (not to mention the other industries and sectors that rely on presentations to get the job done).

The latest trend across all facets of technology seems to be cloud computing and web-based applications. This is closely linked to open source computing and networking. Everything we do these days depends heavily on the Internet, and the world of presentation design and management is no different. Some promising applications that will revolutionize the way you design your presentations—if you let them—have recently appeared. And the gripping fear you feel while waiting to see if your laptop will synchronize with the projector? That could change, too.

ENTER SLIDEROCKET

SlideRocket.com is a small presentation web site that is changing the world—or at least the world as presenters know it. Smart design always answers the most important questions first, and in presentations the first and best question (from our perspective) is always, "How do I get the most out of my deck?" SlideRocket's answer begins with the most basic solutions (like making sure that you're able to actually use the deck—anywhere, anytime) before getting into the simple, functional elements, like designing slides for public viewing.

We depend on technology for nearly everything we do, which is amazing when you consider how often it fails us. Computers crash, batteries fail to charge, programs don't convert, and files corrupt. Murphy's Law rules the digital age with an iron fist. To be fair, technology also streamlines everything we do, making communication and execution simpler and more effective than ever before. But how do we harness the good without encountering the bad?

SlideRocket allows you to utilize their web-based presentation design applications online. You don't download anything to your computer, which means that although you'll need an Internet connection to use it, your presentation's success doesn't depend on a single, fallible technological device. You're welcome to save copies of your final presentation deck to your computer, a memory stick, or any other portable storage device that's designed to help presenters everywhere hedge their bets on technology (and lightening your luggage load when traveling). If you can't access the Internet, you've got your computer or memory device; if your computer fails, you can access the deck from any computer with an Internet connection. Deck display doesn't depend on software editions or file types, either; everything is online, so if you can access SlideRocket.com, you can deliver your presentation as intended.

SlideRocket easily facilitates collaboration on projects and presentations as well. The presentation, as well as any related files or documents, is stored on SlideRocket's server. Anyone with an account (the site has both free and subscription-based options) can access and contribute to the final product. In a world where business partners may live on opposite coasts (or continents), working together on presentations without constantly wrestling with e-mail servers, kickbacks, file archiving and compressing, and so on, can be a real relief. The amount of time high-powered business executives spend trying to surmount the terrestrial limitations of programs like PowerPoint or Keynote may be the most condemning fact in a sea of complaints against those programs.

The web-based application at SlideRocket does all the same things that PowerPoint can do, so you don't have to worry about getting halfway through a presentation project only to discover that you can't upload an image or use a particular font—or discover on presentation day that slide 12 has that galling broken JPEG icon and that you have to explain, in words, how hilarious or emotionally resonant the image was. No one will get it.

SlideRocket even has a limited database of stock photos, making it easier than ever to design a presentation using the previously discussed visual communication strategies. You'll find animations, 2D and 3D transitions (my 3D admonitions pertain to complicated content and imagery, not literal, three-dimensional displays), and many other design elements necessary for the modern presentation. At times, you may need to bolster your capabilities by transitioning from a free account to a fee-based account. This allows additional memory space and an array of premium features that allow you to personalize your presentation and make it shine. However, whichever account type you select, you should find SlideRocket's capabilities to be quite extensive.

Finally, you can use SlideRocket without abandoning PowerPoint if necessary, since PowerPoint files can be uploaded and converted into web-based, SlideRocket form. If you're comfortable and satisfied with PowerPoint, this feature can still help with remote collaboration and provide a web-based presentation delivery option, just in case.

While there are some other competitors out there—280slides .com being the most notable—I've personally found SlideRocket to be the most useful. As someone who enjoys watching technology advance, though, I find it extremely beneficial to check on other programs and applications periodically. If free markets encourage competition and benefit consumers, then the Internet is like marrying the circus with the Olympics: a forum where new, crazy, and sometimes impressive feats of human ingenuity and strength are constantly on display. SlideRocket may be on top right now, but new developments and improvements are distributed to the public at lightning-fast speeds in the modern era. Sticking with whatever program came installed on your computer may be comfortable, but you may find that branching out could breathe new life into old, boring presentations.

GET OUT OF LINE

Though SlideRocket's benefits are numerous, in the grand scheme of things, we need to treat it like a logical, up-to-date improvement on PowerPoint or Keynote. Web capabilities are great, but there's no fundamental revolution of the way we design presentations here. It's slide after slide, template after template.

Then there's Prezi.com, another web-based presentation design application. Communication is almost always done in linear fashion. This makes sense, because you say, "Hello" in one moment and "Goodbye" in another (usually later) moment. Whatever happens in between has taken place chronologically. But what if the basic concepts you're putting forward aren't linear, chronological, or so neatly organized?

Prezi's favorite example is mathematics: We learn counting, the basics (addition, subtraction, multiplication, division), algebra, geometry, calculus, and so on, in that order. We treat counting as if it's separate from calculus, algebra as if the rules don't apply to geometry. Of course, this isn't so. All of these subjects are part of a greater system of mathematics; all of them are intertwined and dependent on one another. Yet we teach math in a linear fashion, thereby treating compartmentalized subjects as part of a very rigid order.

Some topics are made for Prezi, and others aren't. The simplest way I can think to distinguish this is to ask yourself a basic question during the outlining process: does a definite, step-by-step approach make the most sense, or do you find it difficult trying to decide which topic to discuss first? If the latter is your problem, Prezi may totally change your life.

Prezi gives presentation designers the opportunity to put their presentations together outside of a linear, page-by-page construct. Instead of making final decisions on content flow, you simply focus on making great individual slides and putting them together in a network of ideas. You're the expert: You get to help the audience see the big picture. What you end up with is a web-like structure with all closely related slides clustered together in relative proximity to the central theme.

Though this may sound to some like a fast track to the insane asylum, imagine the latitude you're given if your content is somewhat nebulous and you're presenting to more than one audience. Think about history: We know that taxation without representation led to the Boston Tea Party, which led to the American Revolution, which led to Walmart. But all of these events were defined by hundreds of parallel events, or even events that happened centuries earlier. Our trusty timelines don't do any sort of justice for illustrating the intricacies of world-changing events, nor will they do any favors for certain presentations.

And what about customization? Are all of your audiences identical? Sometimes. But what if you have to deliver your presentation to various recipients with different motivations and interests? Let's say you work in finance. For a given presentation, you might have to cover issues like fiscal responsibility, investment track records and professional history, current market trends, and projected growth rates. While that order may work best for potential clients, what if potential financial partners don't *want* to know your professional history? What if a prospective insurer is only interested in fiscal responsibility? Or what if, knowing your audience, you have a gut feeling that you need to start with projected growth rates to get their attention before addressing your own character and pedigree?

Trying to shake up your presentation flow using traditional, linear presentation design software would cause an irrevocable tangle. Trying to jump to slide 36 then back to slide 15 before moving on to slide 45 is not only difficult to remember; it's practically schizophrenic. Prezi provides you with the capability to zoom out and see the big picture, select your destination, and dial straight in. When it's time to move to a different concept, you can zoom out, select, and repeat. Meanwhile, your audience is able to see how each concept relates to the other, creating an underlying understanding of the subject matter that doesn't depend so much on chronology or A + B = C logic. If you've never considered abandoning the timeline when designing your presentation, I highly suggest visiting Prezi.com and taking a look. Again, it's not for everyone: for many presentations, the established linear logic model is best. But if you've wrestled with your content and design for days or weeks to no avail, it's possible that you need to take a markedly different approach.

DECISIONS, DECISIONS

For many presenters, trying to decide between PowerPoint and Keynote, SlideRocket and PowerPoint, or anything and Prezi is going to be a little bit like figuring out the difference between blue cheese and Gorgonzola. Who cares? Just eat the cheese. However, adopting this perspective is like saying you don't believe in love or that you won't clap your hands no matter how ill Tinkerbell is. In short, it makes you a monster.

Before you were even a wink in the air between your father and mother, you were destined for one of these programs. If you try all of them and still don't have a preference, see a therapist: it has more to do with your ability to experience emotions than with the programs' weaknesses.

Discovering the ideal program for your presentation aspirations is one of those unique, only-you-can-know-what's-right decisions. It's okay to be traditional: You raised your first presentations with PowerPoint, so how could you possibly dream of trading 20-plus years of time together—some good, some bad—for some glamorous young web application? But we're not talking about people here; we're talking about computer programs. And don't

PRESENTATIONS ARE

ENORMOUS
opportunities;

FEELING
comfortable & confident
WITH YOUR DECK DEPENDS IN
LARGE PART

ON THE
program
YOU USE TO BUILD IT.

you resent the PowerPoint episode in Philadelphia when your presentation went down in flames due to file corruption? What better vengeance than to ditch the old hag and go online with your future decks?

All of these programs have flaws. Prezi has limited design capabilities, and you need to be fairly savvy with the interface before hopping on stage with a Prezi deck; otherwise, the only thing you'll communicate is mass vertigo that most likely ends in synchronized vomiting. We know the risks associated with PowerPoint and Keynote, and to get the most out of SlideRocket you may have to overcome the technological reticence of more traditional co-workers.

Comfort is king. Designing quality presentations is all that really matters. One of these programs is going to help you maximize your own capabilities, which is the real benefit of trying all of them. Find the one that is easiest for you to understand and utilize, then ask for its hand in marriage. Presentations are enormous opportunities; feeling comfortable and confident with your deck depends in large part on the program you use to build it. Once you've settled down with a nice, sweet presentation design program, it's on to the final step: mastering your delivery.

Chapter 11

Buckets and Butterflies

Doctors will prescribe anxiety medications for just about anything. They're all the rage these days, fitting nicely into a lifecycle of creature comforts that starts with bottles of milk and ends with Metamucil. Acceptable reasons for anxiety medication? Any—and I mean any—concerns about the future, both warranted or contrived.

A cursory glance at the fine print on any anxiety medication reveals the relative limitations of these palliatives. Rarely, if ever, will a pharmaceutical company recommend their miracle pills for the following scenarios: A lion has backed you into a corner, and a T-bone is taped to your jugular; a piano is falling from the sky and, gripped with terror, you have the impulse not to run, but to locate and ingest your anxiety medication; your toddler is running through the house with scissors and, though protected by his replica Batman costume with real vital organ shields, you stupidly forgot to don yours this morning; and worst of all, you wake up unable to breathe and your idiot cat simply will not move from your face, and you cannot scream.

No, anxiety medications are no help in any of the above situations. It's no coincidence: Fear and anxiety are two separate emotions. Whereas fear is an emotional reaction in the face of immediate danger, anxiety is more of a mood or clinical syndrome that stems from the anticipation of future problems. It's characterized by persistent pessimism and is rooted in a lack of control (or just the feeling thereof).

I can't categorically promise that fear should not be included in the cocktail of emotions we all imbibe before public performance. In truth, I've heard of presentations so dull that crowds rush the stage, apprehend the offending speaker, and throw him or her into the nearest body of water (usually located in or around Boston, where dull speech evokes the keen and aggravating memory of powdered wigs and tyranny). But I can say that—with reasonable crowds, content, and delivery—fear of public speaking is not the emotion we're trying to master. We're trying to master anxiety. (Note: I am not trained in mental health. Consult a licensed mental health practitioner before ceasing efforts to master fear. For instance, if you are actually in a corner facing a lion and a T-bone is indeed taped to your neck, please set this book aside and attempt to remove the steak. Then call your doctor, not necessarily in that order.)

This will hopefully come as good news to many of you. Under the strict definition of the word "fear," even if the threat of real harm or danger is imagined, the perceived consequences are extremely near at hand. Mastering fear, then, is going to be maladaptive for the majority of human civilization. Fear provides us with the very logical impulse to run very fast, jump very high, or quickly put on replica superhero attire. Generally speaking, you really shouldn't try to master your fear.

The thing about anxiety is that the worst-case scenario always occurs sometime later.

THE THING ABOUT
anxiety
IS THAT THE
WORST-CASE SCENARIO

always
OCCURS SOMETIME
LATER.

Sure, you could lose your job after giving a bad presentation. Your anxiety in the days leading up to that presentation is always hypothetical; the threat doesn't exist until the presentation has been given. Fear in this scenario is unmanageable: You should be afraid during the long walk to your boss's office after you delivered a poor presentation, lost the account, and now sense immediate, occupational danger. Anxiety totally hinges on what could happen if the presentation doesn't go well. Those are two hypothetical events, one of which is totally controllable: If you feel anxious, you have time to improve.

Nothing takes the emotion out of emotions like mathematics. I find that my level of anxiety almost always has a strong, inversely correlated relationship to my level of preparedness. The more prepared I am, the less anxious I am. Usually, if I practice a presentation eight times before delivery, I don't feel anxious at all. Thus, my simple, heart-of-stone equations: Anxiety = Unprepared. Prepared = 8(Practice). Therefore, 8(Practice) = Unanxious.

(While my childhood goal of becoming the world's foremost emotional mathematician was foiled when I discovered MIT had no such department, I'll trust my readers to realize the encouraging genius in the above display of my raw talent.)

Though anxiety may be separate from fear, it is certainly a gateway emotion. The longer we feel anxious about a possible result (rather than *doing* something about it), the more likely we are to have reason to fear those results. We can spend time eliminating anxiety through extra work, preparation, and commitment, or we can wallow in pessimism about what may occur and just wait for it to happen. You know the old Western trope where the bandit ties the damsel-in-distress to the railroad tracks? Well, that's anxiety, only there's no rope. We're just lying there, and if we don't want to be obliterated by a train, we just need to walk off.

I'm not saying your emotions don't matter. I'm very concerned about your emotions, and I want you to feel like someone cares. All I'm saying is that presentation anxiety isn't worth your time. Preparedness = 8(Practice). There are many highly effective, tangibly calming anxiety reducers on the market today that you won't even need a prescription to try. Here are some of my favorites.

TOP 10 OVER-THE-COUNTER ANXIETY REDUCERS FOR PRESENTERS

10. **No apologies!** This one applies to the presentation moment and any last remnants of anxiety you may be feeling. Apologizing on stage for stuttering, coughing, getting lost for a moment, or any other mistake makes you feel weak and servile—not the sort of person we want to be our expert on anything. Mistakes are going to happen, so forget your manners on stage. No apologies, ever!

9. **Stand on their shoulders:** Morbid psychopaths aside, most of the individuals attending your presentation are looking for real, substantial value. Have you ever watched someone fall to pieces on stage? I've seen audience members in terrible discomfort, not knowing where to look or where to put their hands as the result of poor presenting. Believe me,

when faced with the choice between watching someone discombobulate and spending an hour learning, laughing, experiencing, and growing personally and professionally, most of us want the latter. They're all rooting for you. Just stand on their shoulders.

8. **Engage your imagination:** When children play basketball, they don't just dribble, shoot, and play defense; they imagine: "I'm Michael Jordan!" before a difficult shot or "I'm LeBron James!" while driving to the basket. They may be little runts, but they feel like a 6'6", 250-lb. basketball machines. You'll even hear them count down, "three, two, one" before shots, imagining that the weight of victory or defeat is even greater than in real life. We adults can do the same thing. Imagine yourself walking on stage with the calm confidence of Steve Jobs; pretend you have mastered your material like a seasoned expert; visualize yourself speaking fluidly, like you're engrossed in conversation instead of giving a sterile speech. When the time comes to do the job, you'll find you feel like you've done this a thousand times. After all, how do you think Michael Jordan got so comfortable taking last-second shots? Three, two, one . . .

7. **Make it your strength:** If you're anxious about falling off of a bike, you have two options: Don't ride bikes, or ride and ride until you're incredible at it. The in-between option, riding only when you have to, is almost guaranteed road rash. Presentations are the same, only we sometimes don't have a choice. If you want to gain certain opportunities or effect change, the only thing to do is present to a group of people. When this is reality, make it your strength: Give small-scale presentations frequently. Teach a Sunday school class; speak at a child's school; deliver toasts at parties and

weddings; coach a Little League team. Opportunities to master the craft are everywhere. Pick one or two that suit you and get busy.

6. **Let the little things guide you:** In the midst of our anxiety, we seldom realize the host of minuscule, perfectionist tasks that can occupy our thoughts as we approach the big day. Details like planning an outfit, doing supplemental research, coming up with some extra-special flourishes, and so on, can do double duty for you, because they keep those idle, often pessimistic thoughts at bay while making your presentation perfect down to the last detail. In the final week before a presentation, turn every idle moment into a productive brainstorming session on how you can make it even better. Few people, even the best, would be able to sit on a couch and think positively in idleness for several days. We all tend to self-destruct when we're lying around, so get up and do something!

5. **Exercise:** Human beings tend to separate our areas of health: the mind, the body, the spirit, and so on. When it comes to feeling good, though, there are no compartments; it's all one feeling, and you either have it or you don't. This is one of the greatest pitfalls presenters face: The week(s) leading up to a presentation can be extremely stressful. Late nights, early mornings, traveling, and other routine-crushers become the norm, and all of a sudden we don't have time for the workout routine that helps us feel strong and confident. After a week or two of crash preparation, we stumble on stage feeling like trash. Don't let it happen to you. No matter how hard you have to work in the days or weeks leading up to a presentation, be absolutely steadfast in making time for yourself every day. Not only is exercise a proven way of relieving stress and anxiety,

WE ALL TEND TO *self-destruct* WHEN WE'RE LYING AROUND, SO **GET UP** & **DO** SOMETHING!

but the pride it instills in people often spills over into other areas—like feeling smart, capable, and organized.

4. **Relax:** Your doctor has been telling you to do this for years, and while it's a great bit of lifestyle advice, I'm speaking specifically in regards to the hour or two prior to delivering your presentation. Whenever possible, try to plan the day of the presentation so that you have ample time to clear your head, wrap up any loose ends, and then breathe very slowly, in and out, for at least 10 minutes. Time it. Good, quality breathing can have a tremendous impact on the quality of your presentation. Taking the time to focus on breathing puts you in control of your heart rate, blood pressure, thoughts, and actions. When you're done, straighten up and walk on stage with confidence.

3. **Know the room:** Whenever possible, I like to get this one done the day before the presentation; if that's not possible, do be sure to do it at some point. Spend some time in the venue before you speak. Walk on stage, yes, but also walk around the room. Experience the size, the view from the back row, and the sound of your speaking voice in the room. Play with the lighting if you can. Figure out where the wires, projector, podium, and screen will be. Learn sooner, rather than later, that the podium is taller than you are and plan your jokes accordingly. Unfamiliar places don't cause anxiety, but they definitely facilitate it. Spend enough time in the room to feel comfortable and aware on the big day.

2. **Know the audience:** Of course, there's no way to become familiar with an audience before the presentation. That's just called an earlier-than-expected presentation. You do, however, have to get to know their motivations, whether

they're coming for humor, truth, or a clever mixture of both, and so on. The more familiar you are with the sort of people you'll be speaking to, the better your presentation will be. Just like unfamiliar places facilitate anxiety, unfamiliar people are often the greatest source of discomfort for presenters. What *are* they thinking, anyway? Answering that question to the best of your ability is key to eliminating anxiety. It doesn't matter if your answer is right, so long as you believe it to be true to the best of your knowledge. Remember, feeling comfortable is being comfortable. If you feel like you know your audience, then for all intents and purposes, you know your audience.

1. **Be Prepared:** Thus we conclude the Top 10 Anxiety Reducers List. It may sound obvious, but you'd be amazed at the number of presenters who wing it each and every day. Not just Career Day speeches at local elementary schools, either. I'm talking big, multimillion-dollar deals where the presentation itself was prepared but the speaker was not. Therein lies a key difference: Thorough, organized content paired with neat and evocative design a presentation does not make. The best presentations occur when those elements are synchronized with a prepared speaker. Don't make the mistake of thinking outlining, organization, and design count as preparation. Yes, serial board member and multimillionaire, I'm talking to you: Get in front of the mirror, get on a mock stage, or practice your delivery in front of a camera or some peers. Whom or whatever you stand before, your final presentation should feel as comfortable as riding a bike (assuming you are extremely familiar with riding bikes so that it is basically second nature.)

SENSEI SENSIBILITY

If you've ever been run down by a gang of glow-in-the-dark, skeleton-suit wearing karate misfits, then you know the real value of finding a sensei—fast. Having a reliable sounding board for your content, design, and delivery is a must-have for conquering anxiety. After all, what is our anxiety most often about? It's not that we might lose our jobs; it's what people will think about us! If we can answer this question before the big day, then we won't have to worry about it at all.

Though *The Karate Kid*'s Mr. Miyagi wasn't the boardroom type or the sensational closer, he understood the human mind and, more importantly, the human soul. In the classic coming-of-age story about a transplanted teen searching for stability, Mr. Miyagi dispensed some advice that could be useful to all of us.

Wax On/Wax Off

Like any smart parental figure, Mr. Miyagi saved the reward—karate skills—for last. Prior to learning any fighting skills, his protégé Daniel had to perform a litany of home equity boosting chores (washing the car, sanding the deck, painting the fence, and so on) before getting what he really wanted. In the process, he developed the raw strength and coordination he would need to make real progress as the karate kid. Painting the fence drilled two key blocking movements into his muscle memory without him even having to think about it.

There are things that you do every day that make you a great presenter. Can you tell a great bedtime story to your kids? What about make people laugh around the water cooler? Try to

THERE ARE THINGS YOU DO
every day
THAT MAKE YOU A
GREAT
presenter.

identify some of your best speaking skills (not public speaking; just speaking) and hone them. If you already have skills, you'll find it much easier to transfer those skills to the stage than to start from scratch.

Hearts and Minds

Mr. Miyagi's wisdom in withholding direct karate instruction is revealed when, in a moment of immaturity, Daniel gets so carried away with a technical display of ability that Miyagi sets him straight, hard. Few setbacks are as humiliating as being decked by the elderly.

Impatience, though, has nothing to do with Miyagi's swift reprimand. He is revealing to Daniel how little success in karate, and in life, depends on technical skill. Excellence is in the heart and the mind, not in the sterile execution of physical movements.

I see presenters take the stage with Daniel's approach all the time. I've witnessed decks that are Twitter-interactive, designed by glamorous design firms, written by speechwriters who never worked for George W. Bush, you name it: They've pulled out all the stops and spent every last penny, and they still fall flat on their face. What happened?

We get so focused on the bells and whistles that we forget what it is that we're doing. I, along with every other superstitious person, can't prove that a sixth sense exists. But I can promise you that your audience will know if you're more concerned with impressing them technically than you are with forming an emotional connection. The difference is subtle—impressed audiences do walk away smiling and happy—but when it's time to sign on the dotted line, the results are dramatic.

No Fear

What if you just accept that some of the presentations you give are going to fail? Sometimes it will be you, sometimes the crowd, sometimes the unfortunate natural disaster that destroys the venue in mid-speech, erasing all record that the presentation ever took place.

Mr. Miyagi taught Daniel as much: Without the pressure to be perfect, Daniel was free to become extraordinary. Sometimes, refusing to acknowledge risk has a way of enlarging it; simply admitting that things might not work out sets us free to get on with doing a really solid, quality job. Tip your hat to the worst-case scenario and get on with your great presentation.

Easier Said Than Done

No doubt many of you are fighting deep feelings of resentment at an author asking you to just stop being anxious. I understand: It's paralyzing and has a way of distorting reality. When you're feeling relaxed, it sounds easy enough to just go for a run, breathe, prepare, or do anything to make it go away. When reality sets in, though, things can get a little trickier.

The bike analogy couldn't be more to the point: Anxiety is always going to be unmanageable if you only face it when you absolutely have to. When we were kids learning to ride bikes, we did it all day, every day. First we did it with training wheels, then with a parent close by, then with 20 lbs. of protective gear, and then freestyle over ramps and ditches. If you want to be the BMX equivalent in the presentation world, you have to build up your poise on stage. I promise you that if the only times you step on stage are the biggest moments, you're going to do more to condition your body to become nervous about public speaking than to be comfortable.

This is the old Pavlov discovery: When we consistently experience an emotion next to a stimulus, it becomes conditioned within us. It's natural to experience nerves and anxiety on the big stage; we're talking about tremendous, life-changing opportunities here. However, pair those two together enough, and all of a sudden you'll start feeling anxious every time you hear the word presentation—just like Pavlov's dogs salivated every time they heard the bell, even after the food was removed.

You have the power to condition yourself. Force yourself to speak when nothing is on the line, when it doesn't matter. Who cares if you botch your Aunt Edna's birthday toast? Didn't she give you that new pair of underwear on your 6th birthday for all to see? A bad toast is revenge; a good toast is a step toward presentation excellence.

Speak, speak, speak; deliver, deliver, deliver. If you're going to be a presenter, be one: Present, and do it often. All of the other tricks of the trade depend on a single, indispensable presentation asset: you. If you are compromised by anxiety, the entire presentation comes unhinged. But no pressure—and anyway, haven't we already mastered that?

Chapter 12

Chatterbox

Confidence is the painted metal door that separates the nerds stuffed in the locker from the jocks doing the stuffing. Having confidence is important—after all, you can't properly detain a nerd in a locker without that door—but knowing how to wield it is paramount. No one takes advice from a feeble advisor, but no one takes advice from an egomaniac, either.

I have withheld a simple truth regarding presentations that may undermine the burgeoning confidence of some novice presenters. This truth has to do with group-think, a phenomenon that happens when large numbers of otherwise manageable individuals come together as an audience to listen to you talk.

The bad news is that they all think they're experts. Not just on your subject matter, but on how they should be reached, what's funny versus what isn't, what constitutes an appropriate catering menu in late August, what a supposed expert keynote speaker (that's you) should wear, and so on. The masses are going to be judging you. I'm sorry; that's just the way it is.

CONFIDENCE

IS THE

painted metal door

THAT SEPARATES THE

NERDS *stuffed in the locker*

FROM THE

JOCKS *that do the stuffing.*

The good news is—well, that actually depends. It may just end up being all bad news. Some presenters set out to own their audience in a way that is almost uncomfortably rooted in mind control. That, in a sense, is the good news: An audience is like a big knife, and group-think sharpens the edge, making it easier for many people to act at once. Where the cutting occurs—and exactly what is cut—well, that's entirely up to the speaker. Some presenters are uncomfortable with this sort of wide-scale puppetry, whereas others feel, for the first time, that they have finally arrived at a place in life where everyone listens as well as their stuffed animals did during childhood.

Okay, it isn't puppetry. But perception is nine-tenths of the law in presentations. If you control perception, you control outcomes. Since outcomes are based on the sum of the mental decisions that the audience reaches and acts upon during your presentation, you are, in a sense, controlling a large group of people's mental processes. Don't get a big head, but it's true.

Unfortunately, there is no Jedi hand wave that makes on-stage performing a walk in the park. Even more unfortunately, there is no little red flash, as in *Men in Black*, that can erase from your audience's memory any regrettable impressions you made during a talk. You have a beginning, middle, and end to your presentation. That which happens, happens: Success cannot be preemptively guaranteed, nor can it be regained after the fact. What remains, then, is the arduous task of actually becoming a good onstage presenter.

Obviously, we're dealing with a constant theme here: there is no substitute for hard work and actually being somebody worthwhile in the presentation world. Long-distance communication has experienced change after change, from the Pony Express to telephone lines to instant messaging to Skype. Journalism has gone from print to television to World Wide Web. Yet despite the unbelievable technological innovation that has characterized the past 50 years or so, presentations have more or less remained the same: They are delivered in person, plain and simple. Slide decks may be glossier, and design may be easier. But the barrier between a presenter and his or her audience was, is, and will always be made of air. It is one of the only forms of mass communication left where this is so.

In this sense, presentations are the last bastion of old school communications. Think of what old school means in other industries: no automation, no robotics, no computers, and no technological crutches. Just people and their big, clunky brains making things happen. I know we use technology in presentations (I address the latest capabilities in Chapter 13), but the overall scenario is decidedly quaint. It's a man-to-audience format that has persisted for thousands of years. Imagine the sort of day you'd be in for if you knew you were about to do some 1950s-style farming. With presentations, we often use the same tactics people have been using for decades, even centuries. Thus, it's time to roll up your sleeves.

The first thing any presenter needs to appreciate when considering the upcoming on-stage presentation is that he or she is an absolute chatterbox; that is, you never stop talking. *Ever*.

I don't care if you're the most introverted, hermetic human ever to walk the planet: If you're going on stage, you are a chatterbox. I don't care if your modus operandi consists of standing mutely on stage while attempting to stare your audience into compliance and, after 45 minutes of silent staring, contracts are passed around for signing and the meeting is adjourned: You are a chatterbox. It doesn't matter what happens on stage; once there, we are all chatterboxes.

The reason is simple, and it goes back to the aforementioned inconvenient truth: the simple act of being in an audience has a way of making individuals bona fide experts in everything. They are looking at you, critiquing your every move: eye twitches, facial gestures, crooked tie, shiny shoes (or lack thereof), and so on. An audience member is just that: one member of a group of people. Anonymity has a way of minimizing introspection. Personal responsibility diminishes when individuals become part of a larger organism. The speaker, however, is clearly differentiated from the crowd. The speaker is a loner. The speaker is judged.

Think about it this way: Every individual carries a bucket of thoughts in their head. Hopes, fears, memories, anticipations, responsibilities; you name it, we think about it. However, when we join a group, we have implicit permission to stop focusing on ourselves. It is tribalism revisited—a return to archetypal antiquity. All of a sudden, the big, powerful brain is freed of the peculiar activities that govern 90 percent of its daily load. We're no longer thinking introspectively, because there is no I or me; there is we, the audience. So what happens with that 90 percent? We're still creatures of judgment—that never changes—and we still have the same brains, so it all comes down to one simple factor: What are we looking at? *That* is what we judge. That is what we do with our big brains. The on-stage presenter is on the receiving end of a vast amount of brainpower that has just been turned inside out.

The majority of presenters underestimate this psychological occurrence. They act as if it couldn't matter less what the state of a briefcase may be or the color of a tie. The attitude stems from democratic idealism: People should pay attention to my ideas, not me. People should base my credibility on past performance. You're right: They should. But unfortunately, they don't.

Managing perceptions in the public sphere comes naturally for some. I've met several presenters who get a real kick out of making a personal science of first and last impressions. Still others require a daily reminder just to tie their shoes in the morning. As with so many other areas, recognizing you have a problem is the first step on the road to recovery. I'm not saying there's anything wrong with *you*. There's just something wrong with your presentation approach if you fail to recognize and operate based on the importance of perception-management details.

Failing to practice your nonverbal delivery is the equivalent of getting on stage without a presentation outline, let alone having practiced. For some, the natural state of our nonverbal communications will do. This is sort of like being born 6'10" with an excellent vertical leap: There's a good chance that you'll make a decent basketball player. Natural skill doesn't guarantee success, but it does provide a lot of the impetus behind it.

H.A.G.

Say hello to **H.A.G.**, a villain's whose name is an acronym for "horrible at gestures." He always makes an appearance when a presenter's physical style is...regrettable.

So, if you're naturally charismatic, congratulations. You're on your way to being a presentation god, and this chapter merely informs you of the things that you are already doing without really thinking about it. For the rest of us, this chapter provides the steps that we can take to bridge the gap between the gifted and the ordinary. Whereas we cannot make the decision to grow an extra foot and learn to jump twice our normal capability, we can stand in front of a mirror and watch our hands, and we can make a checklist of appropriate preparations for every on-stage opportunity and pragmatically check them off, one by one.

The best place to start is with the basics: hygiene and attire. The guiding logic is that no amount of smooth body language will overcome a stained burlap sack of a suit and greasy, reeking hair. Yes, it's social convention: You're being forced to comply with a set of arbitrary guidelines that tamp down on individualism across the globe. If this offends you, then I am so sorry—and your cabin in the woods awaits you.

Because I don't want any of you showering in your suits, let's look at hygiene first. Surely, you are already doing some of these things already. But you might be surprised at what can matter.

Facial Hair (Men *and* Women) and Other "Shaveables"

Hairy faces and bodies need not be scorned. They merely reflect one's intimate connection with personal ancestry, an admirable quality that indicates solid roots.

But hair—be it on the head or elsewhere—is an odd material that, like acacia thorns, tends to be messy in its most unaffected state.

Like any natural material, it holds oils, which in turn hold other particulates like dirt and cheese puff residue. Being relatively lightweight, hair does not always submit to the governance of gravity and has a tendency to come untethered. At best, this is distracting. At worst, it is proof that the wild-haired individual is very, very distant from the person who invented Barbasol.

In the 1800s, a full beard was distinguished in even the highest societies; today, the race to manufacture the first 10-blade safety razor makes the race to Mars look like child's play. Untrimmed beards are for mountain men and cannibals. It may be your thing, a trademark of sorts; however, as a general rule, we're shooting for neatly trimmed beards or clean-shaven visages. Anything in between is no-man's-land, so if you want facial hair at all, you'll need to plan ahead by starting a week or more in advance.

To the womenfolk out there, I'm sorry to say that facial hair just won't do. I feel bad saying it because, in a perfect world, we'd all be free to be you and me. But until society progresses to a greater level of acceptance and love, you'll need to keep trimming if you want to present well on stage.

All parties should be mindful of the neck, chest, and back hair that have a way of debuting on certain specimens. You cannot achieve that authoritative *Miami Vice* look without a healthy swath of chest hair in the open V of your favorite shirt, so I'm not saying you need to get rid of it; just keep it neat. If you're searching for more specific guidelines, take a poll of trusted women (ensuring that at least two don't have chest hair fetishes).

Leg hair can be categorically disregarded because you shouldn't be wearing shorts on stage in almost any presentation scenario imaginable. More on that later.

Hygiene

Truth be told, there's actually more leeway in the area of personal hygiene than there is in any other element of nonverbal communication. Being onstage means that you are beyond a breath's-length from the nearest listener and, with the exception of intensely volatile body odor, far enough away from the nearest nose so as not to offend any olfactory senses.

Bear in mind that this leeway assumes that you won't be working the crowd before, during, or after the presentation. It also assumes that you are so generally lazy with your hygiene that it doesn't affect your confidence whatsoever. For many individuals, feeling clean and well groomed translates to power and confidence on stage. Protecting your own senses is part of the game.

So what, really, are we talking about here? Hair, teeth, skin, and fingernails. Technically, we could include clothing maintenance to a certain degree, but we'll save that for the section on style. Since most individuals are willing to comply with social standards, we're also talking about planning for interruptions in a normal hygiene schedule.

Your hair should be neat and washed. Your teeth should be brushed (recently) and as white as possible without being fluorescent. Your skin should be as clear as possible and visibly clean (also, avoid excessive tans and sunburns where applicable; this means planning ahead during the summer speaking schedule). Your fingernails should be manicured and clean. It doesn't matter whether you go into a salon or do it yourself: You'd be surprised at how many members of the top brass club are looking at fingernails for the ultimate measure of hygiene.

Most of you are doing these things already. Good. Just remember to plan ahead for the events that make hygiene difficult to achieve. Lost baggage, delayed flights, and other travel mishaps can derail a suitable appearance faster than any other factor. Here are some basic tips for staying clean on the road.

1. Keep a security checkpoint–approved toiletry bag in your carry-on. No matter what happens, you'll have a toothbrush, toothpaste, deodorant, and soaps.
2. Explore emergency shower options prior to traveling anywhere. Knowing that a venue has shower facilities comes in really handy when your flight is delayed and you no longer have the chance to stop by the hotel.
3. Join the YMCA or some other nationwide club. Nearly every city in America has a YMCA, and every YMCA has shower facilities and lockers. Having an option other than your hotel for pit stops has been extremely useful for me at times. You may feel like a wanderer, but you'll be clean.
4. Pack one more presentation-ready outfit than you need and keep it in a carry-on bag. Even if an audience knows why you're giving your talk in the dingy, crumpled suit you slept in last night, it still comes across as unprepared.

There are millions of business travel tips and tricks out there, but the end goal is simple: Make sure that, no matter what happens, you are able to step on stage feeling clean, fresh, and confident. We can't control what happens, but we can control how we prepare. Don't let outside forces botch your presentation before it's even begun.

WALKING THE STYLE TIGHTROPE

Style discussions are tricky because personal attire serves more than one purpose. It keeps us out of prison, hides our flaws, and provides a basic level of protection from the environment. It also communicates who we are and how we see ourselves to others, as well as how we would like to be seen. This latter sense of style means that your fashion sensibility is as much billboard as anything, an opportunity to advance your personal brand to a group of people.

As such, I can't make across-the-board statements about what should be worn in a presentation. Being the sixth guy on stage at a conference donning a charcoal gray suit and blue tie can be as damaging as being the only guy on stage in a Hawaiian shirt, cargo shorts, and Birkenstocks. It really depends on the situation. If your professional platform is teaching people to run a successful business from home, then those Birkenstocks may communicate the level of freedom you enjoy in your own occupation—proof that you're living the dream. If you want people to listen to the message, not the messenger, then that gray suit will really go a long way toward looking professional but not flamboyant.

Every presenter needs to think critically about the brand they want to display. Is the set of qualities wrapped up in your physical

EVERY PRESENTER

needs to think

CRITICALLY

ABOUT THE

brand

THEY WANT TO DISPLAY.

body and brain a pivotal element of your message, or are the two unrelated? Defining yourself through style is an extremely easy way to provide an audience with immediate context clues as to how they are supposed to listen and engage.

My advice, then, really only pertains to presenters whose message is king. This is the majority of business presenters, politicians, and any other presenter whose purpose is wrapped up in what he or she *does*, rather than how he or she does it. Entertainers, authors, philosophers and the like often have the bulk of their message wrapped up in themselves and must do the hard work of cultivating a style that suits them.

For starters, let's talk clothing.

Color

Color is key, both for presenting a healthy-looking version of you and for achieving situation-appropriate style. As a general rule, navy and gray suits will be your most conservative, business-appropriate colors. Navy tends to look more crisp, whereas gray—especially darker shades—travels better, hiding the incidental spills that seem to be unavoidable while on the road. Thus, if you're speaking the same day as your arrival, a gray suit may be the best choice. Otherwise, pick your favorite.

Browns, olives, and tans tend to be empathetic colors—they're good for human resources representatives, hiring and firing, and any other activities where achieving empathy and mutual understanding are paramount. These colors tend not to be authoritative or powerful, though, so be careful using them on stage.

Black is almost always best reserved for the most formal presentation events. In past times, a black suit was a day-to-day standard in the financial world, particularly on Wall Street. But clearly, past times were more formal than our present time. Situations calling for black will be accordingly infrequent.

Of course, these are very basic rules. Coordinating suits with shirts and ties, plaids with stripes, and shoes with all of the above is an art as deep as you're willing to dive. Skin tone plays a key role in how clothing looks once worn—red or pale skin tones do best with navies and grays; warmer complexions fare well with navies and earth tones. But in every category, the complexity goes much deeper. So how do we get it right?

There are entire books on appropriate business dress—*Dressing the Man* by Alan Flusser or *The Little Black Book of Style* by Nina Garcia are must-reads—but we're presenters, not fashion magnates. Some people don't like the idea of asking for help, but it signifies a very respectable reality: we spend our entire lives attempting to be experts in our fields. Shouldn't we be comfortable letting someone who spends more time in fashion than we do give us counsel?

For men, this is sometimes as easy as consulting a wife, girlfriend, or daughter. But it's dangerous to assume that all women are style experts; have you seen some of the women walking around lately? As many females are confused about good style as males, so choose your advisors carefully. Truly expert advice, often found at reputable local clothing stores, is often free of charge and helps you get back to curing cancer or whatever it is you do. If you don't know whom to trust, hedge your bets by paying attention to the world around you. Maybe GQ and *Detail* magazines are too edgy for you—we can't all be 21 with rippling abs—but what about *Forbes* or *Entrepreneur*? Paying attention to what successful leaders are wearing will help you achieve a basic level of awareness that can shed light on the difference between good and bad advice.

What to Wear

Business style has become undeniably casual in the past several decades. This is partly due to the lax standards of the dot-com startups during the 1990s and partly due to the rapid increase in telecommuting and work-from-home jobs. In the midst of so much "business casual," it can be difficult for a presenter to know what to wear to the big event. Overdressing, for some, is looked down upon as stodgy and outdated. Underdressing, for others, is a cardinal sin and completely disrespectful. You have a 50/50 shot at getting it right—not good odds when something significant is on the line.

So why not just ask? We frequently forget that this is an option and instead put mountains of pressure on our shoulders as we try to guess what is and isn't appropriate. Save yourself the agony: No one will discredit you for being the one to ask. It's practical, it saves time, and it communicates that you have better things to do than sit around postulating about garb guidelines for an upcoming presentation. Call the event coordinator and ask what people will most likely wear to the event. There will almost certainly be a spread, from casual to business casual or business casual to suit and tie. Always land on the more formal side of the spread and get on with your life.

Maintenance

Everything in your possession is a reflection of you. Shoes, briefcases, wallets, purse, and any other accessories you carry can demonstrate your professionalism or your lack of organization. If you're inherently disorganized, you don't have to become someone else to be a good presenter. You just need to put together an organized and respectable presentation. If you don't make your bed when you leave for the big presentation, fine. Just make sure your briefcase is age appropriate (no monogrammed backpacks from high school) and your shoes are shined. Start thinking about the details; those are the elements that people notice. Details separate individuals from one another and provide the most obvious clues about who you are personally.

The First Impression

We all know by now that we have seven seconds to make a first impression. Depending on where you are seated when being introduced, that time frame includes your walk to the stage, navigation of the stage stairs, and first utterances. So what are you going to do with those seconds?

Let's assume that, while people are rapidly coming to conclusions within the first seven seconds of seeing you, they actually spend the first minute or two finalizing their thoughts and cementing them in their brains. The rest of your presentation depends upon a good introduction, so what can we do to make sure it is absolutely riveting?

Obviously, planning ahead really helps. Consider their expectations: What do they usually hear? Who are they usually listening to at presentations? While you absolutely want to communicate warmth and kindness from the stage, qualities like humor, inspiration, expertise, or other qualities depend on your subject matter and objectives. Whatever you do, whether it's going for a laugh or for tears, catching an audience off guard is essential to sidestepping minds and reaching hearts.

Any audience's number one expectation of a speaker is that he or she will speak. I've never presented to an audience that didn't fully expect me to open my mouth and form words in patterns that make sense to human ears. You can't show up at a speaking engagement and not speak, right?

Well, therein lies your first point of authority: No one else is allowed to speak; you are in complete control. If you don't speak, no one does, which means the room is completely silent. Silence, if you haven't noticed, can be uncomfortable—and becomes increasingly so with time. We think a lot about how we're going to use our words, but very little about how we use the absence of them. Silence can be very powerful.

I've experimented with this before. I once arranged my slide deck at the beginning of a presentation to speak for itself. The images were clear and to the point, and any text that appeared was concise and purposeful. The narrative was there, with or without me. Rather than narrating the story line, I simply clicked through the slide progression until reaching the conclusion (in this case, a punch line). To my surprise, the audience laughed. They got the whole thing, and I hadn't even opened my mouth. Furthermore, they were completely engaged with the slide deck because I took myself out of the picture.

Though this is an extreme example of using silence, it really shows the latitude we have in creative presentation tactics. The primary thing I *don't* want to do when I stand up in front of an audience is exactly what they're expecting. I want to get them outside of normal because, most of the time, normal is why I'm giving the talk. Normal is not doing business with my firm and I want to change that. Normal is giving routine presentations, and I want to change that. Normal is not good enough for me; I want to change that.

What will normal get you during your presentation? What does safety get you? Humans are fascinating creatures: we like mountains, we like volcanoes, we like rushing rivers, we like oceans. The dynamic is thrilling; normal is routine.

On the opposite end of the spectrum is talking right away. Skip the introduction: Move it to the middle or the end, for instance. After all, what could be more boring than your name, where you're from, and what you do? Those are the three most stock bits of information you could produce to a group of strangers, yet that's how 99 percent of presentations begin. You're basically telling audience members that you're just like everyone else. Your entire presentation may be designed to prove that you're different, but you'll be fighting that first impression all the way.

Skipping the standard introduction changes everything. I've seen this done in many different ways—opening with a quote, asking a question, posing a problem or statistic—but my favorite method is beginning with an artifact. You need something interesting and completely analogous to the presentation topic; otherwise, you're gambling with irrelevance. But by moving the focus from yourself to thoughts, the business at hand, or an object, you take a dynamic step toward deciding what the audience's focus will be during the presentation—and it won't be you!

The simple act of holding an unexpected object in your hand accomplishes the task of redirection. The audience expects you to step on stage and be the pompous ego that fills their eardrums with humming for the bulk of the near future. Even if their expectations aren't half that pessimistic, they're still not great. However, once they see that something other than a laser pointer or slide clicker is in your hands, their curiosity is immediately piqued.

Curiosity is the little bird that a presenter holds in his or her hands. For as long as the presenter possesses it, the audience cares about him or her. The presenter can nurture it and, ultimately, provide the sought-after answers that satisfy this primal yearning for information. Your artifact, whatever it may be, cultivates curiosity immediately.

CLOSING A TALK

First impressions, especially good ones, are fragile. Closing a discussion well is as vital to your presentation as opening one with style. Some of the tactics can be the same. For instance, one of

the most powerful iterations of the artifact tactic I have ever seen was a closing tactic at the end of a presentation at a dull convention. A family values expert walked on stage with a giant plush panda bear, set it next to the podium, and then proceeded with his presentation as if everything were completely normal. He looked normal enough and his slide deck was normal, also.
He went through an almost academic lecture format discussing various family statistics, but as boring as that sounds, I listened to him more intently than I had to any of the other presenters. Every sentence could have been the one explaining the reason for the big panda bear—was it his Woobie? Was there a bomb inside it? Was it a prize for an audience member? I couldn't figure it out.

He began to conclude his discussion, wrapping up some of the academic concepts he had proposed and providing the action points to the audience, but then he paused. After looking around the audience, he began to talk about family relationships. He talked about his own family and how every decision each family made resulted in a compromise or sacrifice for the other family members. He explained that his son had missed the opportunity to visit the zoo that weekend because he had been preparing for a professional engagement—the very presentation he was giving at that moment. It was a compromise, and he had gotten the large panda bear as a thoughtful substitute for his son's sacrifice.

It was a profound personalization. His message, which had dealt in the statistical evidence that families are drifting apart as individual family members find it easier to pursue individual interests, felt real. I didn't just understand that my choices impact the lives of my loved ones; I felt it. I felt for the speaker's son's missed zoo visit, but I also felt for the speaker. I fully appreciated his commitment to what he was saying, since he clearly felt torn being away from his family over the weekend. To this day, I think about how my decisions affect my loved ones more vividly than I ever had prior to hearing this speaker.

I don't think the message would have had half the power had he told this story at the presentation's beginning. By allowing the audience's curiosity to build, he elevated our capacity for emotional feeling—a required state for catching the heart of his particular message. Revealing the sentiment behind the data he pounded us with at the end of the presentation was pivotal to imparting what was inside his heart to others.

Closing is all about filling people with purpose: your purpose, their purpose, and the reason for the meeting, product, or events being discussed. By planning your presentation well, you should be able to deliver a solid climax to a story that has built throughout the entire talk.

But what do you do with your nonverbal communication?

To get an answer for this, watch some sermons or other powerful political or religious speeches. You'll often find that at the end, the speaker often assumes a much more empathetic, relational posture. The voice, once powerful and authoritative while setting key points in stone, becomes calm and understanding. Instead of being distant on stage, perhaps behind a lectern, the speaker moves to the edge of the stage or out among the audience for closeness. He or she revisited the main points, but with an

THE
BODY—
the thesis, the objectives,
the key points —
IS THE **message;**

THE
CONCLUSION
IS THE **speaker.**

emphasis on the passion behind them and how imperative it is that the audience act on the objectives set forth in the speech.

Why this structure—power and authority in the middle, empathy and compassion at the end? It's simple: The way we close our presentations determines how people think of us once we're gone. The conclusion forces a different perspective of the issues. The body—the thesis, the objectives, the key points—is the message; the conclusion is the speaker. It's how the speaker feels, a chance for him or her to become a human to the audience, rather than a separate entity. In a sense, the conclusion breaks the trance of group-think: It takes individuals out of that audience mind-set and back into personal accountability for the message. When the speaker turns personal, the audience does too. It's a natural, empathetic response—one that can be called upon when it counts.

Conclusion

What you do when you speak, speaks volumes. You are what you think about, but all of your possessions, all of your little quirks and tics, are the result of thoughts you've been thinking for years. The physical representation of your personality is a powerful presentation tool, one that you should be wielding with great force on stage. Start paying attention to the little things: They reveal more about who you are than all of the things you've been telling people about yourself. You are a chatterbox. It's time to take charge of what you're saying.

Chapter 13

Spread the Love

One of the things I hate most about the speaking circuit is the "circuit" part. I'm passionate about my presentations: Each message is like a child that I have personally raised to be a model adult citizen. My messages are smart, athletic, good looking, and sensitive. And though I love my presentations, I don't always love the delivery circuit.

I set out on the road with a message and stop in some city to deliver it. Maybe 50, 100, or even 1,000 people show up. I pour out my heart and soul to these people, pack my bags, and hit the road. It's the nature of serial presenting; it's the lifestyle many of us lead.

I don't hate the experience. I love traveling. I love meeting audience members and sharing my passion with others. I love having the unique opportunity to change the world, one presentation at a time. What I don't love are the obvious limitations that this approach imposes.

I won't name cities, but there are some places I just don't intend to visit. Nothing against small towns, but it's rare that a significant

I'M
passionate
ABOUT MY
PRESENTATIONS:

each message is like a

child

THAT I HAVE

personally raised

TO BE A

model adult citizen.

audience comes together in the remote of Kentucky. And I have a rule about speaking engagements in offshore casinos. I just won't do it.

Then there's my body. I have what you might call "time and space" abnormalities. I've always been rooted to both. Unlike some other presenters who are able to juggernaut across the globe and history in a disjointed, science fiction wonderland of public speaking influence and effectiveness, my presentation success has been limited (for the most part) to the number of places I am willing and able to visit and speak in. I like work, but I do it to support the life I want to live. I don't want to spend my entire life on the road.

So, when presentation opportunities abound, but you share my "time and space" abnormalities, what do you do? You find a way to be everywhere, all the time.

When we talk about presentation delivery, we immediately envision lecterns, microphones, projectors, convention centers, and uncomfortable chairs—all of the things we experience when we attend a presentation. I'm here to tell you that this massive collection of associated memories only pertains to one part of delivering your presentation to audiences. Furthermore, the physical presentation event can occasionally represent just the tip of the iceberg compared with how many people your message could reach.

I'm talking about taking your presentation online. For years, presenters have been doing so using a variety of applications—applications that have, for the most part, been largely uninspiring due to their incomplete nature: They portray the slide deck but not your voice, presence, or both. Thus, you become forced to build a presentation in the previously abolished text-heavy format or to leave your audience in a mystified state by pressing forward with your Godin or Lessig method deck sans explanatory monologue. Or, you just don't go online and abandon the countless individuals who might benefit from hearing your message but can't attend one of your in-person events.

While we've been wrestling with definitions of marriage for humans, the commonplace web acts of Slidesharing and Podcasting got married and had a baby. That baby is Slidecasting, and it changes everything. By pairing your voice with your slides, you can put your little hand in the crook of Opportunity's arm and follow it wherever it goes. Whereas a gathering of two to three potential clients doesn't always justify a trip to Japan, you now have the capacity to treat them to the full measure of your presentation experience via the Web. You've worked hard on your deck; brainstorming, outlining, designing (or paying someone to design), and so on; shouldn't you put that deck to work wherever and whenever possible? I feel confident the logic speaks for itself. For many, the only questions are, How hard will this be? and How do I do it?

SLIDECASTING: THE HOW-TO GUIDE

1. Turn on your computer.
2. Visit a slidecasting web site, like SlideShare.net.
3. Upload your presentation to the site.
4. Record your voice delivering the presentation.

5. Upload the MP3 recording to the Web.
6. Link your slidecast to the MP3 recording (the site will have simple instructions for doing this).
7. Edit your deck so that the slides change in time with your voice.
8. Sip on a margarita while cancelling those mid-winter plane tickets to Warsaw.

There. You've done it. Now, you can capitalize on opportunity right away. Your deck proves that you are the best because of A, B, and C, which you're now able to explain to people from the comfort of your slippers and robe. Of course, slidecasting doesn't replace the physical presentation; it just increases your potential audience from the maximum capacity of the venue as set by the local fire marshal to thousands or millions. No big deal.

My more insecure readers are beginning to wonder just how they are going to get more than a handful of people to care about their presentation. It's a fair question: after all, the Internet is as good at circulating garbage as it is at elevating the little man to the big stage. And no, I don't think your presentation is garbage. I simply mean that differentiating yourself from the vast multitudes out in cyberspace is a completely foreign art to many successful businesspeople today. But that doesn't get you off the hook.

The Internet and its minions (social media, search engines, communications channels, and so on) follow a single guideline (I think) that can help you determine your course of action online: Buzz begets buzz. This is one of those unsolvable mysteries, like how the universe began, why chocolate is so good with peanut butter, and why Macaulay Culkin had to grow up. Many individuals have a lot of buzz going on, but everyone started with nothing. Buzz brings you more buzz, but you basically start out by faking your own notoriety.

Twitter, Facebook, and your blog (please get one) are indispensable assets for you as you press forward with your audience-enlarging schemes. Unfortunately, you'll need to know people—business associates, acquaintances, clients, random people—which is yet another strike against the aspiring public speaking hermit. I'm sorry: The more I think about it, presentation success is not for recluses.

The more you build your network, the more people might see your presentation. But how do you really generate more views?

Incorporating social media and modern technology into your presentation is a surefire approach to generating real, meaningful buzz on the Web regarding your presentation, message, brand, or anything else you want to advance in the public realm. I mentioned this in the chapter on reaching Millennials. With each passing month, a greater percentage of every audience will possess a smartphone that is constantly accessing the Web, while more and more members of your audiences are going to be fighting the urge to return the favor by updating the Web on the trivial details of their daily lives. So why not use this reality to your advantage? Dole out your Twitter tag name and take a poll or survey during your presentation. Have individuals post a comment on a blog you've posted pertaining to the subject at hand. Instead of telling them about your web site, walk them to it by asking them to take out their devices. You'll prevent unsightly episodes of iPhone withdrawal even as you shamelessly promote yourself and whatever it is you are doing.

The Internet has a way of recognizing and spreading these efforts. If you allow them to, interested and engaged members of your audiences will share content—even your presentation, if you've already posted it on SlideShare.net—with their networks. The opportunities are endless—even more so if you've created a truly inspiring message and deck.

I know it sounds easier said than done, but at the end of the day, one's successful web presence is predicated on frequency and buzz. The more active you are in these social media channels, the more you will reap from your use. Morning talk shows are filled with so-called experts on a variety of social topics who literally knighted themselves through the savvy promotion of a random blog idea. It's one of the most reliable ways of getting a book deal, public speaking engagement, or other media appearance today. Limiting your delivery to the physical stage is a profound injustice if your message is truly important. Get on SlideShare.net and start slidecasting. The world is waiting!

TWITTER AND FACEBOOK

Social media outlets come and go, and the study of social media in the twenty-first century is already a major at certain universities. Far be it for me to eliminate from consideration the multitude of innovative, potentially world-changing web outlets that are burgeoning in our current moment, but we're all best served in almost every scenario to go with the outlets that are most ubiquitous: Twitter and Facebook.

Nearly every modern human being has an account with one or both of these web sites. These sites are used with a varying degree of proficiency and frequency, but from our standpoint, we're really focused on the scale of the opportunity, not the level of engagement.

These outlets are useful for every portion of the presentation process, and the simple act of using them enhances the overall potential of the final speaking event. When I'm preparing a presentation, I almost always solicit feedback and input on both Twitter and Facebook—everyone loves having the opportunity to be an expert—and I generate buzz surrounding my topic as the conversation ensues. I'm often able to solicit some very novel ideas free of charge, which significantly cuts down on my overall brainstorming time and budget. As the presentation comes together, I can solicit feedback and input as often as I like, from nailing down content to achieving the perfect design. If you're really brave, you can post videos of your practice presentations: You'd be surprised how gregarious and insightful your followers can be.

Publicizing appearances through social media helps secure a solid turnout for the actual presentation. It also extends the life of the presentation beyond the confines of the speaking engagement, ultimately increasing the return on invested time and resources. I even use these outlets for posting materials, blog articles, or other resources that expound on concepts I just didn't

WHEN WE PRESENT TO AN

audience,

WE'RE ASSUMING A

SUPPORTIVE,

ALMOST

parental

ROLE ON STAGE.

WE'RE SAYING,

"I have the answers to the problems you are facing."

have time to cover during the presentation. It's an extra service I can provide for audience members that extends the one-on-one touch that began during my presentation. When we present to an audience, we're assuming a supportive, almost parental role on stage. We're saying, "I have the answers to the problems you are facing."

That's a powerful assertion and a compelling basis for a relationship. Why let that connection drop when you put the microphone down? If you've put together a stellar presentation, the audience is likely going to value your input in many different areas. Who knows what opportunities could come about if you were able to transition your presence from the stage to the Internet?

TWITTER AS A BACKCHANNEL

Presentation adventurers are increasingly employing Twitter as a backchannel while delivering their presentations. If you're unfamiliar with how this works, you've probably seen it before since many popular cable news outlets do this, too. The commentator breaks from the show's narrative for a bit to address an ongoing Twitter discussion where users are able to ask questions, make points, or otherwise participate with the programming, as opposed to idle listening.

Whether or not to use Twitter in this manner is a personal decision every presenter needs to make based on the subject matter and the circumstances surrounding the presentation. For complicated subjects or engagements where problem solving is a primary objective, the backchannel is extremely useful for a presenter trying to keep a finger on the audience's pulse. The more questions start popping up in the backchannel, the more you know you need to slow down and provide your points in a more thorough manner. You'll also know when the audience doesn't believe a claim you've made or is skeptical about something. Maybe that's good; maybe that's bad. In the end, it comes down to how important you feel it is to know what audience members are thinking.

I'm an optimist; I tend to believe the best about people. But I'm not so crazy as to assume my audience is going to behave appropriately in the backchannel. If you don't regularly watch *The Daily Show with Jon Stewart* or *The Colbert Report,* then you may have missed this trend, but CNN is frequently mocked for the lewd or outrageous comments that sometimes appear on their backchannel discussion boards. When we open up a forum that preserves anonymity, we're bound to get some mischief. Sometimes, the benefits outweigh the risks. Some presenters may not feel confident enough to manage a backchannel like this while trying to deliver meaningful material to the same audience. If you're going to try it, I really recommend doing so in a no-stakes presentation. See how things go before putting something on the line.

You can mitigate many of the risks of using Twitter as a backchannel through preparation. By soliciting input, questions, and concerns from the prospective audience prior to the speaking engagement, you should be able to get a decent idea of what content you need to cover. When audiences feel as though a presentation is heading in a meaningful direction, they're far more likely to participate productively rather than destructively. Prior engagement also lessens the novelty of the exchange, which in turn increases the likelihood that any comments made will be sincere thoughts or questions, rather than idle chatter.

The benefits of this approach should be obvious enough: the audience is engaged in an unprecedented manner. If solving a problem is the presentation's goal, you'll have everyone in the audience working together on that problem. You'll get the credit for having facilitated a powerful brainstorming session on the fly while educating and advancing the discussion with your own expertise.

The risks, however, can be severe as well: If you're not very technologically savvy, it can be quite embarrassing to fumble with the forum on stage before ultimately abandoning the venture. People will feel like you asked for their input but didn't listen to their answers. Your message—the most important element—may become disjointed or confusing if you're unable to focus on both the delivery and the backchannel at the same time. Again, this is an extremely powerful presentation tool, but it is advanced and requires a certain level of proficiency to work just right.

Cliff Atkinson, author of *The Backchannel*, has written at great length on this subject. If you're really interested in pursuing the opportunities of a truly "live" presentation, I suggest you pick up this book. Employing this tool on stage is for the brave, the well prepared, or the soon-to-be-jobless: Make sure you fall into one of the first two categories.

CHANGE THE WORLD, REMEMBER?

Tech-savvy folks never blink at another opportunity to take a part of their lives online, while others get exhausted shortly after logging into Windows and need to rest their eyes. No matter what technology brings to the table, there is still this reality: Presentations are the same as they always have been. It's you, your message, and an audience. It's personal. It's exhilarating. It's a chance to change your world.

I never want people to feel like they can't be successful at presenting because they're uncomfortable implementing one aspect of good, quality presenting. If you feel something is necessary but can't do it yourself, delegate it. Have an intern, assistant, or tech-savvy team member run your Twitter backchannel, freeing you up to be the expert on stage. Or don't use Twitter as a backchannel. Presenting is about the audience: Don't ever compromise your ability to connect with them by attempting to do something you're not good at.

The best presentations begin, in the outline phase, with a clearly defined objective. That objective guides the content, the design, and even the delivery of the presentation. For certain individuals in certain scenarios, the objective will require social media efforts and a live Twitter backchannel. For others, after reviewing and considering the objective, those elements will merely be distractions.

A presentation god is an expert at generating feeling. He can reach his hand out and touch hearts without using a scalpel. These social media strategies are incredible because, when used correctly,

A

presentation

GOD

IS AN EXPERT AT GENERATING

feeling.

HE CAN REACH HIS HAND OUT &

touch hearts

WITHOUT USING A

SCALPEL.

LOW EXPECTATIONS MAN

Watch out!
Low Expectations Man
is your worst enemy!

they really do engender a powerful feeling that only a sense of community can inspire. But we never want to put the cart before the horse: The strategies serve the message, always.

We're out to change the world. We're out to change our lives. We're out to change other people's lives. If you need more exposure, social media has a lot to offer. If you need a stronger connection with your audience, there's a way to do it online. If your message is good but could be great if you just knew how to tap into their minds, social media has a way. Put your presentation on Slideshare. Start using Twitter and Facebook to connect with everyone you know. More importantly, take a deep look at the message you're carrying around. If you had known all along that thousands upon thousands of people might hear it, would you have done something differently? Would you have said something differently? Our worst enemy is our own low expectations. What if the opportunity at hand is far, far bigger than anything you could have imagined? What would you do?

Don't just make a living. Change the world.

Chapter 14

100 Percent All-Natural Passion

To do and to be: These are the actions that define great presentations. Do a set of practical tasks: Brainstorm, outline, design, practice, and speak. Be a set of qualities: confident, charismatic, calm, prepared, and insightful. The quest to build, design, and deliver great presentations comes down to these two simple verbs: do and be. Do everything right, and be absolutely incredible.

Everything in life, in fact, boils down to these two verbs. They answer a single, vital question: Who am I? It's 2011 and we have thousands of years of history to serve as a guide for how we ought to live our lives. We have both good and bad examples. However, we get so caught up in our day-to-day activities that we forget how many of our questions have already been answered by other people in other times. How should I live? What do I want? Where do I find meaning and purpose? The answers are so simple, they're almost unsatisfactory: I am what I do. I am what I am.

The great men and women of history are great because of what they did and what they stood for. Greatness isn't given even to those who inherit thrones on the basis of blood; how many sons of kings have disappeared from the pages of history with barely a mention? Likewise, how many paupers have risen up to redefine the very shape of human existence? Everything that we know about what should and should not be is irrelevant. Everything that we have been up to this very moment is irrelevant. The message we carry, the business we've built, the products we manufacture—all of these things are insignificant until our work is done. We will all be judged by generations of humans that do not yet even exist. In other words: we still have *time*.

If kings can be forgotten, the forgettable can still become kings. Yesterday's failures and abysmal presentations persist only when we fail to replace them with loftier achievements and greater efforts. Every morning is an opportunity to redefine our own existence, to change what we do and who we are, both now and forever. We can spend our time questioning the higher purpose of our lives; however, knowing that we'll never know, we ought to simply get to work advancing our best guesses. No one has any reason to know better than you or me how this world ought to be. In the end, what comes about comes about because some individuals stood up and tried very, very hard to change their world, and others didn't.

We cannot save the world. Presentation gods don't wield final justice. But our efforts can build legacies upon which our families can stand, achievements that prop up generations of people. What you do every day matters. Life is for the living, so who among us is going to live? I intend to advance my causes (not just my cause for better presentations, but everything I care about)

IF
kings
CAN BE
FORGOTTEN,

THE
FORGETTABLE
CAN STILL BECOME
kings.

because I know and trust myself. The values and qualities you hold in your heart are worth sharing and imparting. Do you know and trust yourself?

Yes, this is an emotional plea. And yes, I'm lecturing people on how to live their lives. I know I'm supposed to be teaching you how to give a great presentation, but that's just the thing: I am. The presentation format hasn't changed in any significant way since the first caveman stood up to address his peers with the most eloquent series of grunts he could muster, stating (I assume), "I have an idea that might help a lot of us avoid being ingested by various large predators." That man changed the world, indeed.

What does it mean for a form of communication to resist change over thousands of years of human existence? What does it tell us about ourselves—about our very nature—that we prefer to be personally addressed by our leaders? Every kind of information that exists could be better communicated in a hundred different ways: every chart, graph, concept, and idea might be more easily conveyed through a take-home pamphlet accompanied with an explanatory DVD. Yet we still come together as groups 30 million times a day to listen to an individual talk. It's primal, and no matter how much we complain and mock the situation, we dignify it over and over again simply by partaking in it.

While newspapers collapse, magazines go bankrupt, television stations merge, and radio bandwidths go to auction, presentations carry on. There is no consolidation, no regulatory body that dictates what is and is not possible from the stage. We all have as much latitude as we have creativity and vision: We can do

WHILE
NEWSPAPERS
collapse,

MAGAZINES
ɢᴏ *bankrupt,*

TELEVISION STATIONS
merge,

&

RADIO BANDWIDTHS
ɢᴏ ᴛᴏ *auction,*

PRESENTATIONS
carry on.

anything we want. All the technological innovations that are swirling around us only increase our opportunities. There is no question as to whether or not presentations will exist in 10 or 20 years. We'll still be stepping on stage with a precious message in our hands. It may be different from the message we carry today, but it will be *our message*, the representation of our personal and professional development up to the moment that we greet the audience. The format has not changed, nor will it: your efforts to perfect your approach will endure for as long as you have the heart and health to change your world.

The ultimate lesson in building, designing, and delivering presentations that dominate is learning how to live. Our minds expand to the extent that we consistently challenge and demand more from ourselves. Creativity, passion, and energy are infinite qualities: We possess each in spades when we organize our lives in such a way as to require them daily. The religion of perpetual increase is not our final destination; ours is a religion of efficacy. Whatever we do, whatever we choose to be, we should do and be those things to the absolute edge of possibility. Like the explorers of old, we, too, will discover that in fact there is no edge, only new worlds and new opportunities.

I say all these things because there is no perfect outline. No image has the power to change hearts and minds. No intonation or inflection has any more authority to bypass uncaring ears than any other. There is no magic way of saying or presenting any idea that has any influence at all without there being a person behind it. We are creatures of desire. We want all sorts of things for ourselves and our families, but the most ardent desire is to love and be loved—plain and simple. Therefore, no presentation has any power at all until a warm, caring, sincere human being delivers it. Audiences perceive these qualities in a million different ways according to a million different context clues and circumstances, making it impossible to create an excellent presentation by concocting some formulaic emotional presence. No, we must remember: There is no magic. Successful presentations require presenters who are willing to throw themselves into life with reckless abandon. Reservation is repulsive; passion is persuasive.

The ability to produce a great presentation is an excellent barometer for how well we are living life. Adages like, "failing forward" and "try until you succeed" may be trite, but they are true. If we don't believe in anything enough to feel compelled to share it from the stage, we ought to examine our lives very closely. Even if you value tolerance and acceptance, and feel everyone should be free to live as they choose, those values ought to be taught if they mean anything at all. The goal is not uniformity. If it were, I'd instruct all of you to obtain some sort of position with Apple, since Steve Jobs seems to have the most presentation momentum right now. We'd all get employee discounts on iPads and all the other gadgets we never knew we needed so badly, and life would be grand. No, this is not our pursuit: our pursuit is a turbulent, thrashing mosh pit of ideas and choices. I want it all presented with fervor and passion. How else can any of us begin to make sense of the world through our own eyes? We have to begin with sight, and good vision requires a proper presentation.

So where is your confidence? Where is your charisma? You may feel that you have less charisma than a homeless rodent with a penchant for garlic cheese and your-momma jokes—that is, that no one wants to be like you. But your life isn't chronological. It just feels that way. Every day is disjointed, and the things you think define you aren't facts; they're habits. Forget everything you know about yourself and ask a simple question: What do I care about? If you have a clear answer to that question, you have charisma. And to the human mind, charisma equals direction: We're all willing to follow someone, so long as we feel we're being taken somewhere important. Confidence and charisma are not inherent qualities; rather, they are the external display of internal passion. Stop trying to be something on the outside and start cultivating your innermost desires. *That* is where great presentations begin.

Relax. Before every presentation, we must relax. Pressure is a false feeling. A 30-year mortgage may be very real, but we find a way to pay it every month. Pressure isn't real; it is merely anxiety—pessimistic thoughts about what might happen. So forget it. Breathe, and focus on the minute-to-minute activities that actually have an impact on the events that unfold in your life.

Maslow's Hierarchy of Needs states that we must fulfill our most basic needs before we can actualize ourselves. Before we can become truly passionate about our ideals, we must eat and drink and sleep. So eat, and drink, and sleep. The being comes from the doing: focus on the little things that make us big things. The most profound legacies rest on very basic achievements like eating, drinking, and sleeping. Nothing is accomplished without first accomplishing simple, everyday tasks. While we focus on anxiety, pressure, and uncertainty, moments that we could have spent living life are flying by. Simplicity, like passion, is internal. It has nothing to do with living in the woods and in perfect harmony with nature, but everything to do with being calm and pragmatically doing the small things that move us toward real living. How you define "real living" is up to you, but the distance between you and your dreams isn't time. It's action. There is no string of minutes to be endured; there is a string of doings that need to be done.

In this book, I've laid out a series of doings that will have a remarkable impact on the palatability of your presentation. In other words, I've armed you with an approach that will keep your passion from tripping on your presentation's feet and keep you out of your own way. But if you don't have passion—if your message isn't pinging around your insides like a pinball—then really, who cares? Why bother? If you're not going to put your heart and soul into the message, you might as well hop up on stage with a single-slide deck and get right down to brass tacks: "I'm so-and-so, and I want your business because: (1) I guess I want my job; (2) my family wants to eat and we need at least a little money to do that; and (3) I don't know, just because." You can gloss it up. You can pay someone to design it. But there's no in-between: If you don't have passion, *that* is how you're presenting. *That* is what audiences are coming away with. Why even bother? Couldn't you at least sleep in or spend the day with a child? If you're not going to build a legacy, surely there is something you can do that is more immediately gratifying than stumbling through some half-assed presentation. Wake up. Get on with life, and save us all some precious time.

Go forth and brainstorm. Rise, and thoroughly outline your thoughts. Design your slides without hesitation or insecurity. Sure, everyone might laugh at you. They can always laugh, but they are in the audience because they need something: information, training, direction, or purpose. A problem solved; a new vision, perhaps. You're going on stage because you have that something. You do. You have what they all need. So stand up. Live your life. Go forth and dominate.

Resources

Founded in 2006, Ethos3, based in Nashville, TN, is a presentation boutique providing professional presentation design and training for national and international clients like Google and Pepsi to branded individuals like Guy Kawasaki.

Please visit any of the links below to learn more about Ethos3 and Scott Schwertly.

Ethos3

A presentation design and training company
www.ethos3.com;
Twitter: @ethos3

Scott Schwertly

Scott's life as a presentation maven
www.scottschwertly.com;
Twitter: @scottschwertly; E-Mail:scott@ethos3.com

Have a question? Give Scott a shout-out!

Index